PRESENT CONCERNS

PRESENT CONCERNS

JOURNALISTIC ESSAYS

C. S. Lewis

EDITED BY WALTER HOOPER

HarperOne

An Imprint of HarperCollinsPublishers

HarperCollins books may be purchased for educational, business, or sales promotional use. For information, please email the Special Markets Department at SPsales@harpercollins.com.

Originally published in the United Kingdom in 1986 by Fount Paperbacks.

FIRST EDITION

Library of Congress Cataloging-in-Publication Data

Names: Lewis, C. S. (Clive Staples), 1898-1963, author. | Hooper, Walter, editor.
Title: Present concerns : journalistic essays / C. S. Lewis ; edited by Walter Hooper.
Description: First edition. | New York, NY : HarperOne, 2017. | "Originally published as Present Concerns in the United Kingdom in 1986 by Fount Paperbacks"
Identifiers: LCCN 2016030649 | ISBN 9780062643599 (paperback) | ISBN 9780062565594 (e-book)
Subjects: | BISAC: RELIGION / Spirituality. | RELIGION / Christianity / Literature & the Arts. | RELIGION / Christianity / General.
Classification: LCC PR6023.E926 P74 2017 | DDC 824/.912—dc23 LC record available at https://lccn.loc.gov/2016030649

23 24 25 26 27 LBC 8 7 6 5 4

CONTENTS

INTRODUCTION VII

I THE NECESSITY OF CHIVALRY 1

II EQUALITY 7

III THREE KINDS OF MEN 13

IV MY FIRST SCHOOL 17

V IS ENGLISH DOOMED? 23

VI DEMOCRATIC EDUCATION 31

VII A DREAM 39

VIII BLIMPOPHOBIA 45

IX PRIVATE BATES 51

X HEDONICS 57

XI AFTER PRIGGERY—WHAT? 65

XII MODERN MAN AND HIS CATEGORIES OF
THOUGHT 73

XIII TALKING ABOUT BICYCLES 83

XIV ON LIVING IN AN ATOMIC AGE 91

XV	THE EMPTY UNIVERSE	103
XVI	PRUDERY AND PHILOLOGY	113
XVII	INTERIM REPORT	119
XVIII	IS HISTORY BUNK?	129
XIX	SEX IN LITERATURE	137

INTRODUCTION

'Who is Elizabeth Taylor?' asked C. S. Lewis. He and I were talking about the difference between 'prettiness' and 'beauty', and I suggested that Miss Taylor was a great beauty. 'If you read the newspapers,' I said to Lewis, 'you would know who she is.' 'Ah-h-h-h!' said Lewis playfully, 'but that is how I keep myself "unspotted from the world".' He recommended that if I absolutely 'must' read newspapers I have a frequent 'mouthwash' with *The Lord of the Rings* or some other great book.

As most of those familiar with Lewis's writings will know, it was the 'news' in newspapers that Lewis thought 'possibly the most phantasmal of all histories'. Several times he showed me the only newspaper I remember being delivered to his house on Sundays. It belonged to his gardener, Paxford, and when Lewis and I read the headlines on that paper we hoped to goodness the news in it *was* phantasmal. In any event, I haven't bothered much with newspapers since the brief and immensely happy period when I was living in Lewis's house. And I have tried to be faithful to his prescription regarding 'mouthwashes'.

I do not want to give the impression that Lewis was a Pharisee. He did not condemn either those who wrote for newspapers or those who read them. Otherwise he would have had to censure himself as all but two of these essays were written for newspapers and magazines. Indeed, they provide us with the most complete picture we have of C. S. Lewis the Journalist. It was a role which suited Lewis admirably, for he possessed to an astonishing degree the gift of saying what needed to be said clearly and briefly. There is another thing which sets this book apart from his others. Most of his works are about Theology and Literature. While some of these pieces touch on those subjects, they were brought together because they are about so many other things. Their very variety helps answer the question 'What else was Lewis concerned about?'

The title of this book was suggested by Jeremy Dyson, President of the Oxford University C. S. Lewis Society. Mr Dyson is much younger than I, and after reading some of these essays he found Lewis's concerns very 'present' to him. However, in writing the footnotes for the book I began to wonder how 'present' Lewis's concerns and interests would be to most people. How many readers have heard of Colonel Blimp? Almost everyone would have known who he was when 'Blimpophobia' was first published. In the end I found the answer very close by. *I* had never found out who Colonel Blimp was until I began editing the essays, but I had long known what Lewis meant by Blimpophobia. The truth is that while some of the outward clothing of the things Lewis wrote about has changed, the essentials in all these essays are as important as they always were. I shall be surprised if the essay 'On Living in an Atomic Age' is not of greater concern today than when it first appeared.

C. S. Lewis the Journalist would not be nearly so well represented were it not for the man who introduced me to 'On Living in an Atomic Age'. He is Gordon Wright of Pye Bridge, Derbyshire, and he wrote to me after discovering 'On Living in an Atomic Age' and 'Three Kinds of Men' cut out of whatever journals they had appeared in and stuck into a copy of a book by Lewis. Mr Wright came to Oxford with these treasures—both new to me. It was not difficult to find the source of the first essay but 'Three Kinds of Men' seemed impossible to track down. However, by following various clues provided by the war-news on the back of the cutting I eventually traced it to *The Sunday Times*. I am deeply indebted to Gordon Wright for his generosity. As so often, I have benefited from the willingness of my friend Owen Barfield to go over my own work. Finally, I am grateful to all those publishers who have allowed me to reprint the essays which make up this collection.

'The Necessity of Chivalry' is Lewis's title for the essay published as 'Notes on the Way' in *Time and Tide*, vol. XXI (17 August 1940), p. 841.

'Equality' is reprinted from *The Spectator*, vol. CLXXI (27 August 1943), p. 192.

'Three Kinds of Men' is reprinted from *The Sunday Times*, no. 6258 (21 March 1943), p. 2.

'My First School' was Lewis's title for his 'Notes on the Way' from *Time and Tide*, vol. XXIV (4 September 1943), p. 717.

'Is English Doomed?' is from *The Spectator*, vol. CLXXII (11 February 1944), p. 121.

'Democratic Education' is Lewis's title for his 'Notes on the Way' from *Time and Tide*, vol. XXV (29 April 1944), pp. 369–70.

'A Dream' is reprinted from *The Spectator*, vol. CLXXIII (28 July 1944), p. 77.

'Blimpophobia' is from *Time and Tide*, vol. XXV (9 September 1944), p. 785.

'Private Bates' is reprinted from *The Spectator*, vol. CLXXIII (29 December 1944), p. 596.

'Hedonics' comes from *Time and Tide*, vol. XXVI (16 June 1945), pp. 494–95.

'After Priggery—What?' is reprinted from *The Spectator*, vol. CLXXV (7 December 1945), p. 536.

'Modern Man and His Categories of Thought' is published here for the first time. It was written at the request of Bishop Stephen Neill (1899–1984) for the Study Department of the World Council of Churches. The essay exists only in typescript and it is dated October 1946. At that time Bishop Neill was Secretary of the Assembly Commission II, and the two movements, 'Life and Work' and 'Faith and Order', had come together to become what was formally constituted as The World Council of Churches in 1948.

'Talking About Bicycles' is reprinted from *Resistance* (October 1946), pp. 10–13.

'On Living in an Atomic Age' is taken from the last issue of the annual magazine *Informed Reading*, vol. VI [1948], pp. 78–84.

'The Empty Universe' is my title for Lewis's Preface to D. E. Harding's *The Hierarchy of Heaven and Earth: A New Diagram of Man in the Universe* (London: Faber and Faber, 1952).

'Prudery and Philology' is reprinted from *The Spectator,* vol. CXCIV (21 January 1955), pp. 63–64.

'Interim Report' is reprinted from *The Cambridge Review,* vol. LXXVII (21 April 1956), pp. 468–71.

'Is History Bunk?' is also reprinted from *The Cambridge Review,* vol. LXXVIII (1 June 1957), pp. 647, 649.

'Sex in Literature' is reprinted from *The Sunday Telegraph*, no. 87 (30 September 1962), p. 8. Introducing the essay was this note from the publishers: 'We are facing a crisis in morals, and nowhere is this more apparent than in the treatment by novelists of sex. Ought we not to recognise that literature, while we hope it may do good, in fact often does harm? Do not those modern novels that take—admittedly sometimes with high artistic motives—abnormal sexual behaviour for their theme, popularise and make fashionable and permissible the abnormal sexual behaviour of their characters? . . . We have invited Dr C. S. Lewis as a critic, a novelist, and a Christian apologist to give us his views on this matter, addressing himself to the further question of what in all this should be the attitude of the law. Here is his article.'

And here are eighteen other articles as well. I hope they will prove to be as tonic and pleasant a 'mouthwash' to others as they are to me.

Walter Hooper
8 January 1986
Oxford

I

THE NECESSITY OF CHIVALRY

The word chivalry has meant at different times a good many different things—from heavy cavalry to giving a woman a seat in a train. But if we want to understand chivalry as an ideal distinct from other ideals—if we want to isolate that particular conception of the man *comme il faut* which was the special contribution of the Middle Ages to our culture—we cannot do better than turn to the words addressed to the greatest of all the imaginary knights in Malory's *Morte d'Arthur*. 'Thou wert the meekest man', says Sir Ector to the dead Launcelot. 'Thou wert the meekest man that ever ate in hall among ladies; and thou wert the sternest knight to thy mortal foe that ever put spear in the rest.'[1]

The important thing about this ideal is, of course, the double demand it makes on human nature. The knight is a man of blood and iron, a man familiar with the sight of

---

[1] Sir Thomas Malory, *Le Morte d'Arthur* (1485), XXI, xii.

smashed faces and the ragged stumps of lopped-off limbs; he is also a demure, almost a maidenlike, guest in hall, a gentle, modest, unobtrusive man. He is not a compromise or happy mean between ferocity and meekness; he is fierce to the nth and meek to the nth. When Launcelot heard himself pronounced the best knight in the world, 'he wept as he had been a child that had been beaten'.[2]

What, you may ask, is the relevance of this ideal to the modern world? It is terribly relevant. It may or may not be practicable—the Middle Ages notoriously failed to obey it—but it is certainly practical; practical as the fact that men in a desert must find water or die.

Let us be quite clear that the ideal is a paradox. Most of us, having grown up among the ruins of the chivalrous tradition, were taught in our youth that a bully is always a coward. Our first week at school refuted this lie, along with its corollary that a truly brave man is always gentle. It is a pernicious lie because it misses the real novelty and originality of the medieval demand upon human nature. Worse still, it represents as a natural fact something which is really a human ideal, nowhere fully attained, and nowhere attained at all without arduous discipline. It is refuted by history and experience. Homer's Achilles knows

---

[2] *Le Morte d'Arthur*, XIX, v.

nothing of the demand that the brave should also be the modest and the merciful. He kills men as they cry for quarter or takes them prisoner to kill them at leisure. The heroes of the Sagas know nothing of it; they are as 'stern to inflict' as they are 'stubborn to endure'. Attila 'had a custom of fiercely rolling his eyes, as if he wished to enjoy the terror which he inspired'. Even the Romans, when gallant enemies fell into their hands, led them through the streets for a show, and cut their throats in cellars when the show was over. At school we found that the hero of the First XV might well be a noisy, arrogant, overbearing bully. In the last war we often found that the man who was 'invaluable in a show' was a man for whom in peacetime we could not easily find room except in Dartmoor. Such is heroism *by nature* — heroism outside the chivalrous tradition.

The medieval ideal brought together two things which have no natural tendency to gravitate towards one another. It brought them together for that very reason. It taught humility and forbearance to the great warrior because everyone knew by experience how much he usually needed that lesson. It demanded valour of the urbane and modest man because everyone knew that he was as likely as not to be a milksop.

In so doing, the Middle Ages fixed on the one hope of the world. It may or may not be possible to produce by the thousand men who combine the two sides of Launcelot's character. But if it is not possible, then all talk of any lasting happiness or dignity in human society is pure moonshine.

If we cannot produce Launcelots, humanity falls into two sections—those who can deal in blood and iron but cannot be 'meek in hall', and those who are 'meek in hall' but useless in battle—for the third class, who are both brutal in peace and cowardly in war, need not here be discussed. When this dissociation of the two halves of Launcelot occurs, history becomes a horribly simple affair. The ancient history of the Near East is like that. Hardy barbarians swarm down from their highlands and obliterate a civilisation. Then they become civilised themselves and go soft. Then a new wave of barbarians comes down and obliterates *them*. Then the cycle begins over again. Modern machinery will not change this cycle; it will only enable the same thing to happen on a larger scale. Indeed, nothing much else can ever happen if the 'stern' and the 'meek' fall into two mutually exclusive classes. And never forget that this is their *natural* condition. The man who combines both characters—the knight—is a work not of nature but of art; of that art which has human beings, instead of canvas or marble, for its medium.

In the world today there is a 'liberal' or 'enlightened'

tradition which regards the combative side of man's nature as a pure, atavistic evil, and scouts the chivalrous sentiment as part of the 'false glamour' of war. And there is also a neo-heroic tradition which scouts the chivalrous sentiment as a weak sentimentality, which would raise from its grave (its shallow and unquiet grave!) the pre-Christian ferocity of Achilles by a 'modern invocation'. Already in our own Kipling the heroic qualities of his favourite subalterns are dangerously removed from meekness and urbanity. One cannot quite imagine the adult Stalkey in the same room with the best of Nelson's captains, still less with Sidney! These two tendencies between them weave the world's shroud.

Happily we live better than we write, better than we deserve. Launcelot is not yet irrecoverable. To some of us this war brought a glorious surprise in the discovery that after twenty years of cynicism and cocktails the heroic virtues were still unimpaired in the younger generation and ready for exercise the moment they were called upon. Yet with this 'sternness' there is much 'meekness'; from all I hear, the young pilots in the R.A.F. (to whom we owe our life from hour to hour) are not less, but more, urbane and modest than the 1915 model.

In short, there is still life in the tradition which the Middle Ages inaugurated. But the maintenance of that life depends, in part, on knowing that the knightly character is art, not nature—something that needs to be achieved, not something that can be relied upon to happen. And this knowledge is specially necessary as we grow more democratic. In previous centuries the vestiges of chivalry were kept alive by a specialised class, from whom they spread to other classes partly by imitation and partly by coercion. Now, it seems, the people must either be chivalrous on its own resources, or else choose between the two remaining alternatives of brutality and softness. This is, indeed, part of the general problem of a classless society, which is too seldom mentioned. Will its *ethos* be a synthesis of what was best in all the classes, or a mere 'pool' with the sediment of all and the virtues of none? But that is too large a subject for the fag-end of an article. My theme is chivalry. I have tried to show that this old tradition is practical and vital. The ideal embodied in Launcelot is 'escapism' in a sense never dreamed of by those who use that word; it offers the only possible escape from a world divided between wolves who do not understand, and sheep who cannot defend, the things which make life desirable. There was, to be sure, a rumour in the last century that wolves would gradually become extinct by some natural process; but this seems to have been an exaggeration.

II

EQUALITY

I am a democrat because I believe in the Fall of Man. I think most people are democrats for the opposite reason. A great deal of democratic enthusiasm descends from the ideas of people like Rousseau, who believed in democracy because they thought mankind so wise and good that everyone deserved a share in the government. The danger of defending democracy on those grounds is that they're not true. And whenever their weakness is exposed, the people who prefer tyranny make capital out of the exposure. I find that they're not true without looking further than myself. I don't deserve a share in governing a hen-roost, much less a nation. Nor do most people—all the people who believe advertisements, and think in catchwords and spread rumours. The real reason for democracy is just the reverse. Mankind is so fallen that no man can be trusted with unchecked power over his fellows. Aristotle said that some people were only fit to be slaves. I do not contradict him. But I reject slavery because I see no men fit to be masters.

This introduces a view of equality rather different from that in which we have been trained. I do not think that equality is one of those things (like wisdom or happiness) which are good simply in themselves and for their own sakes. I think it is in the same class as medicine, which is good because we are ill, or clothes which are good because we are no longer innocent. I don't think the old authority in kings, priests, husbands, or fathers, and the old obedience in subjects, laymen, wives, and sons, was in itself a degrading or evil thing at all. I think it was intrinsically as good and beautiful as the nakedness of Adam and Eve. It was rightly taken away because men became bad and abused it. To attempt to restore it now would be the same error as that of the Nudists. Legal and economic equality are absolutely necessary remedies for the Fall, and protection against cruelty.

But medicine is not good. There is no spiritual sustenance in flat equality. It is a dim recognition of this fact which makes much of our political propaganda sound so thin. We are trying to be enraptured by something which is merely the negative condition of the good life. And that is why the imagination of people is so easily captured by appeals to the craving for inequality, whether in a romantic form of films about loyal courtiers or in the brutal form of Nazi ideology. The tempter always works on some *real* weakness in our own system of values: offers food to some need which we have starved.

When equality is treated not as a medicine or a safety-gadget but as an ideal we begin to breed that stunted and envious sort of mind which hates all superiority. That mind is the special disease of democracy, as cruelty and servility are the special diseases of privileged societies. It will kill us all if it grows unchecked. The man who cannot conceive a joyful and loyal obedience on the one hand, nor an unembarrassed and noble acceptance of that obedience on the other, the man who has never even wanted to kneel or to bow, is a prosaic barbarian. But it would be wicked folly to restore these old inequalities on the legal or external plane. Their proper place is elsewhere.

We must wear clothes since the Fall. Yes, but inside, under what Milton called 'these troublesome disguises',[1] we want the naked body, that is, the *real* body, to be alive. We want it, on proper occasions, to appear: in the marriage-chamber, in the public privacy of a men's bathing-place, and (of course) when any medical or other emergency demands. In the same way, under the necessary outer covering of legal equality, the whole hierarchical dance and harmony of our deep and joyously accepted

---

[1] John Milton, *Paradise Lost* (1667), Book IV, line 740.

spiritual inequalities should be alive. It is there, of course, in our life as Christians: there, as laymen, we can obey—all the more because the priest has no authority over us on the political level. It is there in our relation to parents and teachers—all the more because it is now a willed and wholly spiritual reverence. It should be there also in marriage.

This last point needs a little plain speaking. Men have so horribly abused their power over women in the past that to wives, of all people, equality is in danger of appearing as an ideal. But Mrs Naomi Mitchison has laid her finger on the real point. Have as much equality as you please—the more the better—in our marriage laws: but at some level consent to inequality, nay, delight in inequality, is an *erotic* necessity. Mrs Mitchison speaks of women so fostered on a defiant idea of equality that the mere sensation of the male embrace rouses an undercurrent of resentment. Marriages are thus shipwrecked.[2] This is the tragi-comedy of the modern woman; taught by Freud to consider the act of love the most important thing in life, and then inhibited by feminism from that internal surrender which alone can make it a complete emotional success. Merely for the sake

---

[2] Naomi Mitchison, *The Home and a Changing Civilisation* (London, 1934), chapter 1, pp. 49–50.

of her own erotic pleasure, to go no further, some degree of obedience and humility seems to be (normally) necessary on the woman's part.

The error here has been to assimilate all forms of affection to that special form we call friendship. It indeed does imply equality. But it is quite different from the various loves within the same household. Friends are not primarily absorbed in each other. It is when we are doing things together that friendship springs up—painting, sailing ships, praying, philosophising, fighting shoulder to shoulder. Friends look in the same direction. Lovers look at each other: that is, in opposite directions. To transfer bodily all that belongs to one relationship into the other is blundering.

We Britons should rejoice that we have contrived to reach much legal democracy (we still need more of the economic) without losing our ceremonial Monarchy. For there, right in the midst of our lives, is that which satisfies the craving for inequality, and acts as a permanent reminder that medicine is not food. Hence a man's reaction to Monarchy is a kind of test. Monarchy can easily be 'debunked'; but watch the faces, mark well the accents, of the debunkers. These are the men whose tap-root in Eden has been cut: whom no rumour of the polyphony, the dance, can reach—men to whom pebbles laid in a row are more beautiful than an arch. Yet even if they desire mere equality they cannot reach it. Where men are forbidden to honour a king they honour millionaires, athletes, or film-stars instead: even famous prostitutes or gangsters. For spiritual nature, like bodily nature, will be served; deny it food and it will gobble poison.

And that is why this whole question is of practical importance. Every intrusion of the spirit that says 'I'm as good as you' into our personal and spiritual life is to be resisted just as jealously as every intrusion of bureau-cracy or privilege into our politics. Hierarchy within can alone preserve egalitarianism without. Romantic attacks on democracy will come again. We shall never be safe unless we already understand in our hearts all that the anti-democrats can say, and have provided for it better than they. Human nature will not permanently endure flat equality if it is extended from its proper political field into the more real, more concrete fields within. Let us *wear* equality; but let us undress every night.

III

THREE KINDS OF MEN

There are three kinds of people in the world. The first class is of those who live simply for their own sake and pleasure, regarding Man and Nature as so much raw material to be cut up into whatever shape may serve them. In the second class are those who acknowledge some other claim upon them—the will of God, the categorical imperative, or the good of society—and honestly try to pursue their own interests no further than this claim will allow. They try to surrender to the higher claim as much as it demands, like men paying a tax, but hope, like other taxpayers, that what is left over will be enough for them to live on. Their life is divided, like a soldier's or a schoolboy's life, into time 'on parade' and 'off parade', 'in school' and 'out of school'. But the third class is of those who can say like St Paul that for them 'to live is Christ'.[1] These people have got rid of the tiresome business of adjusting the rival

---

[1] Philippians 1:21.

claims of Self and God by the simple expedient of rejecting the claims of Self altogether. The old egoistic will has been turned round, reconditioned, and made into a new thing. The will of Christ no longer limits theirs; it is theirs. All their time, in belonging to Him, belongs also to them, for they are His.

And because there are three classes, any merely twofold division of the world into good and bad is disastrous. It overlooks the fact that the members of the second class (to which most of us belong) are always and necessarily unhappy. The tax which moral conscience levies on our desires does not in fact leave us enough to live on. As long as we are in this class we must either feel guilt because we have not paid the tax or penury because we have. The Christian docrine that there is no 'salvation' by works done according to the moral law is a fact of daily experience. Back or on we must go. But there is no going on simply by our own efforts. If the new Self, the new Will, does not come at His own good pleasure to be born in us, we cannot produce Him synthetically.

The price of Christ is something, in a way, much easier than moral effort—it is to want Him. It is true that the wanting itself would be beyond our power but for one fact. The world is so built that, to help us desert our own satisfactions, they desert us. War and trouble and finally old age take from us one by one all those things that the natural Self hoped for at its setting out. Begging is our only wisdom, and want in the end makes it easier for us to be beggars. Even on those terms the Mercy will receive us.

IV

MY FIRST SCHOOL

'Next week would be no good,' said the boy. 'I'm going back to school on Friday.' 'Bad luck,' said I. 'Oh, I don't know,' said the boy. And stealing a look at his face I saw that this was not stoicism. He really didn't mind going back to school; possibly he even liked it.

Was it merely envy of a generation happier than my own which filled me with a vague distaste at this discovery? One must not dismiss the possibility too lightly. The spirit that says 'I went through it, why shouldn't they?' is a strong one and clever at disguises. But I believe I can, on this occasion, acquit myself. I was feeling, in a confused way, how much good the happy schoolboys of our own day miss in escaping the miseries their elders underwent. I do not want those miseries to return. That is just where the complexity of things comes in.

My first preparatory school was one of the last survivals

of the kind depicted in *Vice Versa*,[1] except for one detail. There were no informers. Whether the hirsute old humbug who owned it would have run the place by espionage if the boys had given him the chance, I do not know. The treacle-like sycophancy of his letters to my father, which shocked me when they came into my hands years afterwards, does not make it improbable. But he was given no chance. We had no sneaks among us. The Head had, indeed, a grown-up son, a smooth-faced carpet-slipper sort of creature apt for the sport; a privileged demi-god who ate the same food as his father though his sisters shared the food of the boys. But we ourselves were (as the Trades Unions say) 'solid'. Beaten, cheated, scared, ill-fed, we did not sneak. And I cannot help feeling that it was in that school I imbibed a certain indispensable attitude towards mere power on the one hand and towards every variety of Quisling on the other. So much so that I find it hard to see what can replace the bad schoolmaster if he has indeed become extinct. He was, sore against his will, a teacher of honour and a bulwark of freedom. The Dictators and the Secret Police breed in countries where schoolboys lack the No Sneaking Rule. Of course one must wish for good schoolmasters. But if they breed up a genera-

---

[1] F. Anstey, *Vice Versa* (1882).

tion of the 'Yes, Sir, and Oh, Sir, and Please, Sir brigade', Squeers[2] himself will have been less of a national calamity.

And then, the end of term. The little pencilled calendar in the desk. Twenty-three days more, twenty-two days more, twenty-one days more . . . this time next week . . . this time the day after tomorrow . . . this time tomorrow . . . the trunks have come down to the dormitory. Bunyan tells us that when the Pilgrims came to the land of Beulah 'Christian with desire fell sick; Hopeful also had a fit or two of the same disease'.[3] How well I know that sickness! It was no mere metaphor. It thrilled and wobbled inside: passed along the spine with delicious, yet harrowing thrills: took away the appetite: made sleep impossible. And the last morning never betrayed one. It was always not less, but more, than desire had painted it: a dizzying exaltation in which one had to think hard of common things lest reason should be overset. I believe it has served me ever since for my criterion of joy, and especially of the difference between joy and mere pleasure. Those who remember such Ends of Term are inexcusable if ever, in later life, they allow mere pleasure to fob them off. One

[2] Wackford Squeers is the headmaster of Dotheboys Hall in Charles Dickens's *Nicholas Nickleby* (1838–39).
[3] John Bunyan, *The Pilgrim's Progress*, ed. James Blanton Wharey, second edition revised by Roger Scharrock (1960), Part I, p. 155.

can tell at once when that razor-edged or needle-pointed quality is lacking: that shock, as if one were swallowing light itself.

But one learned more even than that. At the beginning of each term the end was incredible. One believed in it of course, as a conventionally 'religious' person 'believes' in heaven. One disbelieved in it as such a person disbelieves in heaven. Consolations drawn from that source availed against the imminent horror of tomorrow's geometry (geometry was the great flogging subject with us) just as much as talk about heavenly glory avails against a worldly man's suspicion that he is getting cancer. The joys of home were, for the first half of the term, a mere 'escapist' phantom. Theoretically there was somewhere a world where people had comfortable clothes, warm beds, chairs to sit in, and palatable food: but one could not make it real to one's mind. And then, term after term, the incredible happened. The End did really come. The bellowing and grimacing old man with his cane, his threats, and his ogreish facetiousness, the inky walls, the stinking shed which served both as a latrine and as a store for our play-boxes, all 'heavily vanished' like a dream.

There was of course a darker miracle. For the first half of the holidays, Term was likewise unbelievable. We knew— would you call it knowing?—that we must go back: just as a healthy young man in peacetime knows—if you call it knowing—that his hand will some day be the hand of a skeleton: or as we all know that the planet will one day be uninhabitable, and (later) the whole universe will 'run down'. But each time the unbelievable came steadily on, and happened. There came a week, a day, an hour when the holidays were over, 'portions and parcels of the dreadful past', as if they had never been. And that is why I have never since been able, even when I held a philosophy that encouraged me to do so, to take quite at its face value the apparent importance of Present Things. I can (quite often) believe in my own death and in that of the species, for I have seen *that kind of thing* happening. I can believe with nerves and imagination as well as intellect, in human immortality; when it comes it will be no more astonishing than certain other wakenings that I have experienced. To live by hope and longing is an art that was taught at my school. It does not surprise me that there should be two worlds.

What is the moral of this? Not, assuredly, that we should not try to make boys happy at school. The good results which I think I can trace to my first school would not have come about if its vile procedure had been intended to produce them. They were all by-products thrown off by a wicked old man's desire to make as much as he could out of deluded parents and to give as little as he could in return. That is the point. While we are planning the education of the future we can be rid of the illusion that we shall ever replace destiny. Make the plans as good as you can, of course. But be sure that the deep and final effect on every single boy will be something you never envisaged and will spring from little free movements in your machine which neither your blueprint nor your working model gave any hint of.[4]

---

[4] In his autobiography, *Surprised by Joy* (1955), Lewis devoted a chapter to his first school which he refers to as 'Belsen'. Its real name was Wynyard School and it was located in Watford, Hertfordshire. Wynyard was sliding into ruin when Lewis went there in 1908, and he won his freedom when the school came to an end in 1910. It was not until after the publication of *Surprised by Joy* that Lewis discovered that the extremely brutal headmaster had long been insane. A year after his school collapsed he died in an insane asylum.

V

IS ENGLISH DOOMED?

Great changes in the life of a nation often pass unnoticed. Probably few are aware that the serious study of English at English Universities is likely to become extinct. The death-warrant is not yet signed, but it has been made out. You may read it in the Norwood Report.[1] A balanced scheme of education must try to avoid two evils. On the one hand the interests of those boys who will never reach a University must not be sacrificed by a curriculum based on academic requirements. On the other, the liberty of the University must not be destroyed by allowing the requirements of schoolboys to dictate its forms of study. It is into this second trap that the writers of the Report have fallen. Its

---

[1] The title of 'The Norwood Report', so called after its chairman Sir Cyril Norwood, is *Curriculum and Examinations in Secondary Schools: Report of the Committee of the Secondary School Examinations Council Appointed by the President of the Board of Education in* 1941 (1943). See also Lewis's essay 'The Parthenon and the Optative' in his *Of This and Other Worlds,* ed. Walter Hooper (1982). The American title of this book is *On Stories: And Other Essays on Literature* (1982).

authors are convinced that what they mean by 'English' can be supplied 'by any teacher' (p. 94). 'Premature external examination' in this subject is deprecated (p. 96); and I am not clear when, if ever, the moment of 'maturity' is supposed to arrive. English scholars are not wanted as teachers. Universities are to devise 'a general honours degree involving English and ... some other subject' (p. 97); not because English studies will thus flourish, but to suit the schools.

No instructed person to whom I have talked doubts that these proposals, if accepted, mean the end of English as an academic discipline. A subject in which there are no external examinations will lead to no State scholarships; one in which no school teachers are required will lead to no livelihoods. The door into academic English, and the door out of it, have both been bricked up. The English Faculty in every University thus becomes a faculty without students. At some of the largest Universities, no doubt, there will still be a Professor of English, as there is a Professor of Sanskrit or of Byzantine Greek, and four or five students (in a good year) may attend his lectures. But as an important element in the intellectual life of the country the thing will be dead. We may confidently hope, indeed, that English scholarship will survive abroad, notably in America and Germany; it will not survive here.

There are some who will welcome this result. English faculties have a habit of being obtrusive. The strongly modernist and radical character of the Cambridge Tripos, and what has been called (with exaggeration) the disquietingly Christian flavour of the Oxford 'Schools', may each, in its different way, offend. Taken together, they are certainly a warning that if you want a mass-produced orthodoxy you will be ill-advised to let the young study our national literature, for it is a realm where *tout arrive;* but I do not think the Report was inspired by such considerations. If it kills English scholarship it will probably have done so inadvertently; its views are the result of honest misunderstanding. It believes that 'any teacher' in the course of teaching his own special subject can teach clear and logical English. The view would have been plausible when the oldest of those who made the Report were themselves at school. For them all teachers had been trained in the Classics. The results of that discipline on English style were not, it is true, so good as is often claimed, but it removed at least the worst barbarisms. Since then the Classics have almost been routed. Unless English, seriously studied, succeeds to their place, the English which 'any teacher' inculcates in the course of teaching something else will be at best the reflection of his favourite newspaper and at worst the technical jargon of his own subject.

The danger is lest the views of the Report should be generally approved (as they were possibly formed) under a misunderstanding of the real nature of English scholarship. Many will think it reasonable to examine children in Geography or (Heaven help us!) in Divinity, yet not in English, on the ground that Geography and Divinity were never intended to entertain, whereas Literature was. The teaching of English Literature, in fact, is conceived simply as an aid to 'appreciation'. And appreciation is, to be sure, a *sine qua non*. To have laughed at the jokes, shuddered at the tragedy, wept at the pathos—this is as necessary as to have learned grammar. But neither grammar nor appreciation is the ultimate End.

The true aim of literary studies is to lift the student out of his provincialism by making him 'the spectator', if not of all, yet of much, 'time and existence'. The student, or even the schoolboy, who has been brought by good (and therefore mutually disagreeing) teachers to meet the past where alone the past still lives, is taken out of the narrowness of his own age and class into a more public world. He is learning the true *Phaenomenologie des Geistes;* discovering what varieties there are in Man. 'History' alone will not do, for it studies the past mainly in secondary authorities. It is possible to 'do History' for years without knowing at the end what it felt like to be an Anglo-Saxon *eorl,* a cavalier, an eighteenth-century country gentleman. The gold behind the paper currency is to be found, almost exclusively, in literature. In it lies deliverance from the tyranny of generalisations and catchwords. Its students know (for example) what diverse realities—Launcelot, Baron Bradwardine, Mulvaney[2]—hide behind the word *militarism.* If I regard the English Faculties at our Universities as the chief guardians (under modern conditions) of the Humanities, I may doubtless be misled by partiality for studies to which I owe so much; yet in a way I am well placed for judging. I have been pupil and teacher alike in *Literae Humaniores,* pupil and teacher alike in English; in the History School (I confess) teacher only. If anyone said that English was now the most liberal—and liberating—discipline of the three, I should not find it easy to contradict him.

'In this time, place, and fortune,' said Sidney's Musidorus, 'it is lawfull for us to speake gloriously'—for he spoke in the condemned cell.[3] If England, departing from the practise of Greece and Rome, is about to banish the systematic study of her own literature, it is an honest

---

[2] Sir Launcelot of the Arthurian Romances; Baron Bradwardine in Sir Walter Scott's *Waverley* (1814); Terence Mulvaney is one of the three privates in Rudyard Kipling's *Soldiers Three* (1888).
[3] Sir Philip Sidney, *The Arcadia* (1590), Book V.

pride to remember before the blow falls what fruits that study has borne during its short existence. They challenge comparison with those of any discipline whatever. We have lived scarcely a hundred years, we English scholars. In that time we have given our country the greatest dictionary in the world. We have put into print a vast body of medieval literature hitherto imprisoned in manuscript. We have established the text of Shakespeare. We have interpreted that of Chaucer. We have transmitted to our most recent poets the influence of our most ancient. We can claim as our own the rich humanity of Raleigh, the more astringent genius of W. P. Ker, the patient wisdom of R. W. Chambers, and (further back) such tough old giants as Skeat, Furnivall, York Powell, Joseph Wright. More recently at Cambridge we have begun an enquiry into the nature of literary experience which has no real precedent later than Aristotle. Most recently of all, at Oxford, we have (first of all Faculties in all Universities) conducted an Examination for Englishmen now behind barbed wire in Germany. We felt, as we read and re-read the answers, which told of so many hours usefully and delightedly passed in prison, that the labour had been immensely worth while. Here, we thought, was an incontestable witness to the value, not simply of 'appreciation', but of a steady march down centuries of changing sentiment, thought, and manners. Here, we thought, was a good augury for the future. We did not yet know that our prize, like Launcelot's, was death.

The Board of Education carries heavier metal than those who are merely scholars and Englishmen. If it resolves to sink us, it can. But it is desirable that a rather larger public should know what exactly it is that is going down.

VI

DEMOCRATIC EDUCATION

Democratic education, says Aristotle, ought to mean, not the education which democrats like, but the education which will preserve democracy. Until we have realised that the two things do not necessarily go together we cannot think clearly about education.

For example, an education which gave the able and diligent boys no advantage over the stupid and idle ones, would be in one sense democratic. It would be egalitarian and democrats like equality. The caucus-race in *Alice*, where all the competitors won and all got prizes, was a 'democratic' race: like the Garter it tolerated no nonsense about merit.[1] Such total egalitarianism in education has not yet been openly recommended. But a movement in that direction begins to appear. It can be seen in the grow-

---

[1] The Order of the Garter, instituted by King Edward III in 1344, is the highest order of knighthood. Lewis had in mind the comment made by Lord Melbourne (1779–1848) about the Order: 'I like the Garter; there is no damned merit in it.'

ing demand that subjects which some boys do very much better than others should not be compulsory. Yesterday it was Latin; today, as I see from a letter in one of the papers, it is Mathematics. Both these subjects give an 'unfair advantage' to boys of a certain type. To abolish that advantage is therefore in one sense democratic.

But of course there is no reason for stopping with the abolition of these two compulsions. To be consistent we must go further. We must also abolish *all* compulsory subjects; and we must make the curriculum so wide that 'every boy will get a chance at something'. Even the boy who can't or won't learn his alphabet can be praised and petted for *something*—handicrafts or gymnastics, moral leadership or deportment, citizenship or the care of guinea-pigs, 'hobbies' or musical appreciation—anything he likes. Then no boy, and no boy's parents, need feel inferior.

An education on those lines will be pleasing to democratic feelings. It will have repaired the inequalities of nature. But it is quite another question whether it will breed a democratic nation which can survive, or even one whose survival is desirable.

The improbability that a nation thus educated could survive need not be laboured. Obviously it can escape destruction only if its rivals and enemies are so obliging as to adopt the same system. A nation of dunces can be safe only in a world of dunces. But the question of desirability is more interesting.

The demand for equality has two sources; one of them is among the noblest, the other is the basest, of human emotions. The noble source is the desire for fair play. But the other source is the hatred of superiority. At the present moment it would be very unrealistic to overlook the importance of the latter. There is in all men a tendency (only corrigible by good training from without and persistent moral effort from within) to resent the existence of what is stronger, subtler, or better than themselves. In uncorrected and brutal men this hardens into an implacable and disinterested hatred for every kind of excellence. The vocabulary of a period tells tales. There is reason to be alarmed at the immense vogue today of such words as 'high-brow', 'up-stage', 'old school tie', 'academic', 'smug', and 'complacent'. These words, as used today, are sores: one feels the poison throbbing in them.

The kind of 'democratic' education which is already looming ahead is bad because it endeavours to propitiate evil passions, to appease envy. There are two reasons for not attempting this. In the first place, you will not succeed. Envy is insatiable. The more you concede to it the more it will demand. No attitude of humility which you can possibly adopt will propitiate a man with an inferiority complex. In the second place, you are trying to introduce equality where equality is fatal.

Equality (outside mathematics) is a purely social conception. It applies to man as a political and economic animal. It has no place in the world of the mind. Beauty is not democratic; she reveals herself more to the few than to the many, more to the persistent and disciplined seekers than to the careless. Virtue is not democratic; she is achieved by those who pursue her more hotly than most men. Truth is not democratic; she demands special talents and special industry in those to whom she gives her favours. Political democracy is doomed if it tries to extend its demand for equality into these higher spheres. Ethical, intellectual, or aesthetic democracy is death.

A truly democratic education—one which will preserve democracy—must be, in its own field, ruthlessly aristocratic, shamelessly 'high-brow'. In drawing up its curriculum it should always have chiefly in view the interests of the boy who wants to know and who can know. (With very few exceptions they are the same boy. The stupid boy, nearly always, is the boy who does not *want* to know.) It must, in a certain sense, subordinate the interests of the many to those of the few, and it must subordinate the school to the university. Only thus can it be a nursery of those first-class intellects without which neither a democracy nor any other State can thrive.

'And what,' you ask, 'about the dull boy? What about our Tommy, who is so highly strung and doesn't like doing sums and grammar? Is he to be brutally sacrificed to other people's sons?' I answer: dear Madam, you quite misunderstand Tommy's real wishes and real interests. It is the 'aristocratic' system which will really give Tommy what he wants. If you let me have my way, Tommy will gravitate very comfortably to the bottom of the form; and there he will sit at the back of the room chewing caramels and conversing *sotto voce* with his peers, occasionally ragging and occasionally getting punished, and all the time imbibing that playfully intransigent attitude to authority which is our chief protection against England's becoming a servile State. When he grows up he will not be a Porson;[2] but the world will still have room for a great many more Tommies than Porsons. There are dozens of jobs (much better paid than the intellectual ones) in which he can be very useful and very happy. And one priceless benefit he will enjoy: he will know he's not clever. The distinction

---

[2] Richard Porson (1759–1808), son of the parish clerk at East Ruston, near North Walsham, showed extraordinary memory when a boy, and by the help of various protectors he was educated at Eton and Trinity College, Cambridge. In 1792 he became Regius Professor of Greek at Cambridge.

between him and the great brains will have been clear to him ever since, in the playground, he punched the heads containing those great brains. He will have a certain, half-amused respect for them. He will cheerfully admit that, though he could knock spots off them on the golf links, they know and do what he cannot. He will be a pillar of democracy. He will allow just the right amount of rope to those clever ones.

But what you want to do is to take away from Tommy that whole free, private life as part of the everlasting opposition which is his whole desire. You have already robbed him of all real play by making games compulsory. Must you meddle further? When (during a Latin lesson really intended for his betters) he is contentedly whittling a piece of wood into a boat under the desk, must you come in to discover a 'talent' and pack him off to the woodcarving class, so that what hitherto was fun must become one more lesson? Do you think he will thank you? Half the charm of carving the boat lay in the fact that it involved a resistance to authority. Must you take that pleasure—a pleasure without which no true democracy can exist—away from him? Give him marks for his hobby, officialise it, finally fool the poor boy into the belief that what he is doing is just as clever 'in its own way' as real work? What do you think will come of it? When he gets out into the real world he is bound to discover the truth. He may be disappointed. Because you have turned this simple, wholesome creature into a coxcomb, he will resent those inferiorities which (but for you) would not have irked him at all. A mild pleasure in ragging, a determination not to be much interfered with, is a valuable brake on reckless planning and a valuable curb on the meddlesomeness of minor officials: envy, bleating 'I'm as good as you', is the hotbed of Fascism. You are going about to take away the one and foment the other. Democracy demands that little men should not take big ones too seriously; it dies when it is full of little men who think they are big themselves.

VII

A DREAM

I still think (with all respect to the Freudians) that it was the concourse of irritations during the day which was responsible for my dream.

The day had begun badly with a letter from L. about his married sister. L.'s sister is going to have a baby in a few months; her first, and that at an age which causes some anxiety. And according to L. the state of the law — if 'law' is still the right word for it — is that his sister can get some domestic help only if she takes a job. She may try to nurse and care for her child provided she shoulders a burden of housework which will prevent her from doing so or kill her in the doing: or alternatively, she can get some help with the housework provided she herself takes a job which forces her to neglect the child.

I sat down to write a letter to L. I pointed out to him that of course his sister's case was very bad, but what could he expect? We were in the midst of a life and death struggle. The women who might have helped his sister had all been diverted to even more necessary work. I had just got thus far when the noise outside my window became so loud that I jumped up to see what it was.

It was the W.A.A.F.[1] It was the W.A.A.F., not using typewriters, nor mops, nor buckets, nor saucepans, nor pot-brushes, but holding a ceremonial parade. They had a band. They even had a girl who had been taught to imitate the antics of a peacetime Drum Major in the regular army. It is not, to my mind, the prettiest exercise in the world for the female body, but I must say she was doing it very well. You could see what endless pains and time had gone to her training. But at that moment my telephone rang.

It was a call from W. W. is a man who works very long hours in a most necessary profession. The scantiness of his leisure and the rarity of his enjoyments gives a certain sacrosanctity to all one's engagements with him: that is why I have had an evening with him on the first Wednesday of every month for more years than I can remember. It is a law of the Medes and Persians. He had rung up to say that he wouldn't be able to come this Wednesday. He is in the Home Guard, and his platoon were all being turned out that evening (all after their day's work) to practise—

---

[1] Women's Auxilliary Air Force.

ceremonial slow marching. 'What about Friday?' I asked. No good; they were being paraded on Friday evening for compulsory attendance at a lecture on European affairs. 'At least,' said I, 'I'll see you at church on Sunday evening.' Not a bit of it. His platoon—I happen to know that W. is the only Christian it contains—were being marched off to a different church, two miles away; a church to which W. has the strongest doctrinal objections. 'But look here,' I asked in my exasperation, 'what the blazes has all this tomfoolery got to do with the purposes for which you originally joined the old L.D.V.?'[2] W., however, had rung off.

The final blow fell that evening in Common Room. An influential person was present and I'm *almost* sure I heard him say, 'Of course we shall retain some kind of conscription after the war; but it won't necessarily have anything to do with the fighting services.' It was then that I stole away to bed and had my dream.

I dreamed that a number of us bought a ship and hired a crew and captain and went to sea. We called her the *State*. And a great storm arose and she began to make heavy

---

[2] The Local Defence Volunteers were organised in May 1940 for men between the ages of 17 and 65. Their purpose was to deal with German parachutists. The name was changed to the Home Guard in December 1940, and conscription began in 1941. (See also the footnote to 'Blimpophobia' on p. 44.)

weather of it, till at last there came a cry 'All hands to the pumps—owners and all!' We had too much sense to disobey the call and in less time than it takes to write the words we had all turned out, and allowed ourselves to be formed into squads at the pumps. Several emergency petty officers were appointed to teach us our work and keep us at it. In my dream I did not, even at the outset, greatly care for the look of some of these gentry; but at such a moment—the ship being nearly under—who could attend to a trifle like that? And we worked day and night at the pumps and very hard work we found it. And by the mercy of God we kept her afloat and kept her head on to it, till presently the weather improved.

I don't think that any of us expected the pumping squads to be dismissed there and then. We knew that the storm might not be really over and it was as well to be prepared for anything. We didn't even grumble (or not much) when we found that parades were to be no fewer. What did break our hearts were the things the petty officers now began to do to us when they had us on parade. They taught us nothing about pumping or handling a rope or indeed anything that might help to save their lives or ours. Either there was nothing more to learn or the petty officers did not know it. They began to teach us all sorts of things—the history of shipbuilding, the habits of mermaids, how to dance the hornpipe and play the penny whistle and chew tobacco. For by this time the emergency petty officers (though the real crew laughed at them) had become so very, very nautical that they couldn't open their mouths without saying 'Shiver my timbers' or 'Avast' or 'Belay'.

And then one day, in my dream, one of them let the cat out of the bag. We heard him say, 'Of course we shall keep all these compulsory squads in being for the next voyage: but they won't necessarily have anything to do with working the pumps. For, of course, shiver my timbers, we know there'll never be another storm, d'you see? But having once got hold of these lubbers we're not going to let them slip back again. Now's our chance to make this the sort of ship we want.'

But the emergency petty officers were doomed to disappointment. For the owners (that was 'us' in the dream, you understand) replied, 'What? Lose our freedom and *not* get security in return? Why, it was only for security we surrendered our freedom at all.' And then someone cried, 'Land in sight'. And the owners with one accord took every one of the emergency petty officers by the scruff of his neck and the seat of his trousers and heaved the lot of them over the side. I protest that in my waking hours I would never have approved such an action. But the dreaming mind is regrettably immoral, and in the dream, when I saw all those meddling busybodies going *plop-plop* into the deep blue sea, I could do nothing but laugh.

My punishment was that the laughter woke me up.

VIII

BLIMPOPHOBIA

It may well be that the future historian, asked to point to the most characteristic expression of the English temper in the period between the two wars, will reply without hesitation, 'Colonel Blimp'.[1] No popular cartoonist can work in a vacuum. A nation must be in a certain state of mind before it can accept the kind of satire which Mr Low was then offering. And we all remember what that state of mind was. We remember also what it led to; it led to Munich, and via Munich to Dunkirk. We must not blame Mr Low (or Mr Chamberlain or even Lord Baldwin) much more than we blame ourselves. All of us, with a very few exceptions, shared the guilt, and all, in some measure, have paid for it.

---

[1] David Low (1891–1963) won great acclaim for his cartoons which appeared in the *Evening Standard* for whom he worked from 1926 to 1949. His most famous creation was 'Colonel Blimp' who was portrayed as a bald, rotund, elderly gentleman delivering himself of self-contradictory aphorisms. He has come to mean a muddle-headed type of complacent reactionary.

For this state of mind many causes might be given; but I want at present to draw attention to one particular cause which might be overlooked. The infection of a whole people with *Blimpophobia* would have been impossible but for one fact—the fact that seven out of every ten men who served in the last war, emerged from it hating the regular army much more than they hated the Germans. How mild and intermittent was our dislike of 'Jerry' compared with our settled detestation of the Brass Hat, the Adjutant, the Sergeant-Major, the regular Sister, and the hospital Matron! Now that I know more (both about hatred and about the army) I look back with horror on my own state of mind at the moment when I was demobilised. I am afraid I regarded a Brass Hat and a Military Policeman as creatures quite outside the human family.

In this I was certainly very wrong. It may even be that the whole war machine of the last war was not in the least to blame for the impression it produced on those who went through it. My present purpose is not to settle a question of justice, but to draw attention to a danger. We know from the experience of the last twenty years that a terrified and angry pacifism is one of the roads that lead to war. I am pointing out that hatred of those to whom war gives power over us is one of the roads to terrified and angry pacifism. *Ergo*—it is a plain syllogism—such hatred is big with a promise of war. A nation convulsed with *Blimpophobia* will refuse to take necessary precautions and will therefore encourage her enemies to attack her.

The danger of the present situation is that our Masters have now been multiplied. This time it is not only the Brass Hat and the Military Police; it is our Masters in Civil Defence, in the Home Guard, and so forth. Signs have already appeared, if not of bitter resentment against them, at any rate of an anxiety lest they should not abdicate, and that completely, at the first possible moment. And here comes the catch. Those who wish for whatever reason to keep their fellow-citizens regimented longer than is necessary will certainly say that they are doing so in the interests of security. But I say that the disappearance of all these Masters at an early date is just what security demands.

If they extend their power too long, or abuse it while it lasts, they will be more hated than any body of Englishmen have been hated by their compatriots since the time of Peterloo.[2] Mr Low—or some successor of Mr Low—will imprint their image indelibly on our

---

[2] Peterloo is the name (a burlesque adaptation of Waterloo) given to a charge of cavalry and yeomanry on the Manchester reform meeting which was held in St Peter's Field, Manchester, on 16 August 1819. It resulted in eleven people being killed, with about six hundred injured.

minds. It will not, of course, be Colonel Blimp this time. Perhaps it will be Mr Mares-Neste. He will be, I think, a retired business man who, having few brains, finds the time hanging heavy on his hands, and, being a bore, is the greatest nonentity in his neighbourhood. The cartoons almost draw themselves. We see Mr Mares-Neste rising, say, in the Home Guard. We see how endless and useless parades, which are an unspeakable nuisance to his more intelligent neighbours, are a perfect god-send to Mares-Neste: here is something to do, here is self-importance. We see him doing things which no officer in the real army would be allowed to do—parading the men without greatcoats in winter while he wears one himself, or practising ceremonial drill in wartime. We see him developing a disquieting tendency to theocracy and becoming fond of church parades, though he himself, perhaps, hardly knows his catechism.

An outrageously false picture, you say? I hope with all my heart that it is. But any prolongation of our Masters' authority beyond the necessary time, or any slightest abuse of it, will quickly bring this nation of freemen into a state of mind in which the picture will be accepted as true. And then the fat will be in the fire. All real and necessary measures for our security will be 'sicklied o'er' with the taint of Mares-Neste. The indignation which finally sweeps him away will, in its haste, reject any and every scheme of compulsory national service. If you want a man to refuse the nasty medicine that he really needs, there is no surer way than to ply him daily with medicines no less nasty which he perceives to be useless.

The future of civilisation depends on the answer to the question 'Can a democracy be persuaded to remain armed in peacetime?' If the answer to that question is No, then democracy will be destroyed in the end. But 'to remain armed' here means 'to remain effectively armed'. A strong navy, a strong air force, and a reasonable army are the essentials. If they cannot be had without conscription, then conscription must be endured. For the sake of our national existence we are ready to endure that loss of liberty. But we are not ready to endure it for anything less. A continued interference with our liberties which sets up, instead of a real army, some such ridiculous and (by itself) useless *simulacrum* as a permanent Home Guard officered by the Mares-Nestes—this, be sure, we will not tolerate. If we pay the price, we shall insist on getting the goods; if we do not get the goods, let no man dream that we shall go on paying the price. That is our present position. But the danger is that if you impose Mr Mares-Neste on us too long, you will make the very name of compulsion not only so hateful but so contemptible that our readiness to pay for real goods will disappear. Bad money drives out good. The Jack-in-Office discredits the fruitful authority. A permanent (or even prolonged) Home Guard will drive us into a frenzied anti-officialdom, and that frenzy into total disarmament, and that disarmament into the third war.[3]

---

[3] On 14 May 1940 the Secretary of State for War, Anthony Eden, broadcast an appeal for all men between the ages of 17 and 65 to enrol in an organisation to be known as the Local Defence Volunteers. Their primary purpose was to deal with the threat of German parachutists, and within a month the new force numbered nearly a million and a half. In July 1940 the Prime Minister, Winston Churchill, altered its name to the Home Guard. Conscription began in 1941 and by December of that year Lewis began his duties with the Home Guard. Many men enjoyed the evening parades and drilling with whatever armament could be scraped together—shotguns, golf clubs, sticks. At times their fervour for catching Germans extended to stopping almost anyone who happened to be out at night. As a result, many people claimed to be more afraid of the Home Guard than of the Germans. Lewis was greatly relieved when the Home Guard received their 'stand-down' on 3 December 1944, which day was marked by a review of representative units in Hyde Park at which King George VI took the salute. That evening the King broadcast the nation's thanks to the Home Guard for their 'steadfast devotion'.

IX

PRIVATE BATES

The habit of taking dramatic characters out of their setting and writing their biographies as if they were real
people is not one which, as a critic, I can commend. But I
have at the moment a special reason—not a literary one—
for thus extracting a character from *Henry V.* He will be
Private Bates.

In one respect Private Bates shared with the modern serviceman the good fortune of serving under a national leader
of heroic mould and dazzling eloquence. Shakespeare's
Henry was as rousing a chief as our present Prime Minister.[1]
His 'pep talks' were about as good as Shakespeare could
make them, which means they were about as good as that
kind of thing can be. It will not be generally thought that
the modern serviceman hears anything better.

What effect this splendid propaganda had on John
Bates, Shakespeare reveals very clearly. He had been told,

---

[1] Winston Churchill.

on the eve of Agincourt, that the King would not wish himself anywhere but where he was. This cut no ice at all with Bates. He replied that, though it was a (blank) cold night, he didn't mind betting that the (blank) King would rather be up to the neck in the Thames than mucking about in the lines at Agincourt, and he added a rider to the effect that if the King did really like mucking about in the said lines, he, John Bates, heartily wished the King could be left to get on with it by himself and let sensible chaps go home. He had also been told that the King's 'cause was just and his quarrel honourable':[2] in modern language, that we were fighting for civilisation against barbarism and to make the world safe for democracy.

It was at this point that another private, one Williams, who had hitherto been just stamping his feet and staring, too 'browned off' to say anything at all, chipped in with what I take to be the Elizabethan equivalent of 'Sez you' or 'Oh yeah'. His actual words were 'That's more than we know'.[3] 'That's right,' growled Bates, and anyway, he added, it was no (blank) business of theirs. They had to obey their (blank) orders; the rights and wrongs of the war were the King's funeral. 'And enough for him to be going

---

[2] *Henry V*, Act IV, scene 1, lines 134–35.
[3] *Henry V*, Act IV, scene 1, line 136.

on with, too,' said Private Williams. Then the conversation drifted on to something like Post-War Policy and the 'implementing' of promises made to the fighting man. The King had promised that he would never be ransomed. 'Yes, *promised*,' said Williams with withering emphasis. 'And if he does go and get ransomed after you've had your throat cut, a (blank) lot *you'll* know about it. *Promised!*' This infuriated the only person present who took the Government's pep talks seriously, and a quarrel developed. But Bates wouldn't stand for that. 'Shut up, shut up!' he said wearily. 'Pair of bally fools. Ain't ye got Frenchies enough to fight without fighting one another? Silly, I call it.'

It would be a pity to leave the scene without noticing that there was another soldier present, Private Court. He said nothing. He is there for the very purpose of saying nothing. No front line conversation would be complete without that silent figure. He says nothing. He knows there is no good in saying anything. He stopped saying things years ago when the war was young and when his illusions were shattered: perhaps after the first promise of leave was broken, perhaps when he discovered that the state of the French army was quite different from what he had been led to expect, perhaps when, in the midst of a headlong retreat, he came across a newspaper which said we were advancing.

Now of course Shakespeare knew no more than we do—perhaps less—about the English soldier in the time of Henry V. But he knew the Elizabethan soldier. This scene gives his answer to the question which has recently been agitating a number of people, the question of 'what the soldier thinks'. And the answer, in the supposedly 'spacious' days of Elizabeth after the defeat of the Armada, was that the soldier thought everything his leaders said was 'eyewash'. Whatever had been recently said in these columns about the scepticism or 'cynicism' of the modern soldier was, according to Shakespeare, at least equally true of the Elizabethan soldier. And Shakespeare does not seem to be specially disquieted by it; the scene occurs not in a satire, but in a heroic and patriotic play about a 'famous victory'.

The Shakespearian evidence suggests that our present disquiet about 'what the soldier thinks' is due not to any temporary deterioration in the soldier's *morale*, still less to any malice or incompetence in the observers, but to the fact that the upheaval of war is permitting, and indeed forcing, members of the more educated (and credulous) classes to see close up what the great mass of the people in this country are, and always have been, like. What they see gives them a shock, because it is so very unlike what they expected. But it is not in itself very dreadful. It might be better: it might be worse.

In the last few years I have spent a great many hours in third-class railway carriages (or corridors) crowded with servicemen. I have shared, to some extent, the shock. I found that nearly all these men disbelieved without hesitation everything that the newspapers said about German cruelties in Poland. They did not think the matter worth discussion: they said the one word 'Propaganda' and passed on. This did not shock me: what shocked me was the complete absence of indignation. They believe that their rulers are doing what I take to be the most wicked of all actions—sowing the seeds of future cruelties by telling lies about cruelties that were never committed. But they feel no indignation: it seems to them the sort of procedure one would expect.

This, I think, is disheartening. But the picture as a whole is not disheartening. It demands a drastic revision of our beliefs. We must get rid of our arrogant assumption that it is the masses who can be led by the nose. As far as I can make out, the shoe is on the other foot. The only people who are really the dupes of their favourite newspapers are the *intelligentsia*. It is they who read leading articles: the poor read the sporting news, which is mostly true. Whether you like this situation or not depends on your views. It is certainly hard on you if you are a Planner or a man with any panacea that demands a nation of united enthusiasts. Your ship will be wrecked on the immemorial, half-kindly, half-lazy, wholly ironic, incredulity of the English people. If you are not a Planner you may feel that this immovable scepticism, this humour, this disillusioned patience (an almost inexhaustible patience—'How differs it from the terrible patience of God!') is no very bad basis for national life. But I think the true conclusion is that the existence of Private Bates in his millions should both stifle your hopes and allay your fears. It is he who makes it improbable that anything either very bad or very good will ever happen in this island. And when all's said and done, he did beat the French chivalry at Agincourt.

X

HEDONICS

There are some pleasures which are almost impossible to account for and very difficult to describe. I have just experienced one of them while travelling by tube from Paddington to Harrow. Whether I can succeed in making it imaginable to you is doubtful; but certainly my only chance of success depends on impressing you, from the outset, with the fact that I am what used to be called a country cousin. Except for a short spell in a London hospital during the last war I have never lived in London. As a result I not only know it badly but also I have never learned to regard it as a quite ordinary place. When, on the return from one of my visits, I plunge underground to reach Paddington, I never know whether I shall strike daylight again at the staircase which comes up under the hotel or at a quite different place out near the end of the departure platforms. 'All is fortune' so far as I am concerned; I have to be prepared for either event as I have to be prepared for fog, rain, or sunshine.

But of all London the most complete *terra incognita* is the suburbs. Swiss Cottage or Maida Vale are to me, if not exactly names like Samarkand or Orgunjé, at any rate names like Winnipeg or Tobolsk. That was the first element in my pleasure. Setting out for Harrow, I was at last going to burrow into that mysterious region which is London and yet wholly unlike the London that country cousins know. I was going to the places from which all the Londoners whom one met in streets and buses really came, and to which they all returned. For central London is, in one deep sense of the word, hardly *inhabited*. People stay there (there are, I gather, hotels) but few live there. It is the stage; the dressing-rooms, the green room, all the 'behind the scenes' world is elsewhere—and that was where I was going.

Perhaps I must labour here to convince you that I am not being ironical. I beg you to believe that all these 'vales' and 'woods' and 'parks' which are so ordinary to Londoners are, to my ear, a kind of incantation. I have never been able to understand why the fact of living in the suburbs should be funny or contemptible. Indeed I have been trying on and off for years to complete a poem which (like so many of my poems) has never got beyond the first two lines—

Who damned suburbia?
'I,' said Superbia.

There is, indeed, only one way in which a Londoner can come to understand my feeling. If it gives him pleasure to see for a moment how London looks to me, then this pleasure—the pleasure of seeing a thing the wrong way round, which makes the magic of all mirrors—is the very same which I get from the mere idea of the suburbs. For to think of them is to think that something to me so unhomely as London is to other people simply home. The whole pattern turns inside out and upside down.

It was early evening when my journey began. The train was full, but not yet uncomfortably full, of people going home. It is important to insist—you will see why in a moment—that I was under no illusion about them. If any one had asked me whether I supposed them to be specially good people or specially happy or specially clever, I should have replied with a perfectly truthful No. I knew quite well that perhaps not ten per cent of the homes they were returning to would be free, even for that one night, from ill temper, jealousy, weariness, sorrow, or anxiety, and yet—I could not help it—the clicking of all those garden gates, the opening of all those front doors, the unanalysable home smell in all those little halls, the hanging up of all those hats, came over my imagination with all the caress of a half-remembered bit of music. There is an extraordinary charm in other people's domesticities. Every lighted house, seen from the road, is magical: every pram or lawn-mower in someone else's garden: all smells or stirs of cookery from the windows of alien kitchens. I intend no cheap sneer at one's own domesticities. The pleasure is, once more, the mirror pleasure—the pleasure of seeing as an outside what is to others an inside, and realising that you are doing so. Sometimes one plays the game the other way round.

Then other things come in. There was the charm, as we went on, of running out into evening sunlight, but still in a deep gulley—as if the train were swimming in earth instead of either sailing on it like a real train or worming beneath it like a real tube. There was the charm of sudden silence at stations I had never heard of, and where we seemed to stop for a long time. There was the novelty of being in that kind of carriage without a crowd and without artificial light. But I need not try to enumerate all the ingredients. The point is that all these things between them built up for me a degree of happiness which I must not try to assess because, if I did, you would think I was exaggerating.

But wait. 'Built up' is the wrong expression. They did not actually impose this happiness; they offered it. I was free to take it or not as I chose—like distant music which you need not listen to unless you wish, like a delicious faint wind on your face which you can easily ignore. One was invited to surrender to it. And the odd thing is that something inside me suggested that it would be 'sensible' to refuse the invitation; almost that I would be better employed in remembering that I was going to do a job I do not greatly enjoy and that I should have a very tiresome journey back to Oxford. Then I silenced this inward wiseacre. I accepted the invitation—threw myself open to this feathery, impalpable, tingling invitation. The rest of the journey I passed in a state which can be described only as joy.

I record all this not because I suppose that my adventure, simply as mine, is of any general interest, but because I fancy that something of the same sort will have happened to most people. Is it not the fact that the actual quality of life as we live it—the *weather* of the consciousness from moment to moment—is either much more loosely or else very much more subtly connected than we commonly suppose with what is often called our 'real' life? There are, in fact, two lives? In the one come all the things which (if we were eminent people) our biographers would write about, all that we commonly call good and bad fortune and on which we receive congratulations or condolences. But side by side with this, accompanying it all the way like that ghost compartment which we see through the windows of a train at night, there runs something else. We can ignore it if we choose; but it constantly offers to come in. Huge pleasures, never quite expressible in words, sometimes (if we are careless) not even acknowledged or remembered, invade us from that quarter.

Hence the unreasonable happiness which sometimes surprises a man at those very hours which ought, according to all objective rules, to have been most miserable. You will ask me whether it does not cut both ways. Are there not also grim and hideous visitors from that secondary life—inexplicable cloudings when all is going what we call 'well'? I think there are; but, to be frank, I have found them far less numerous. One is more often happy than wretched without apparent cause.

If I am right in thinking that others besides myself experience this occasional and unpredicted offer, this invitation into Eden, I expect to be right also in believing that others know the inner wiseacre, the *Failer*, who forbids acceptance. This Jailer has all sorts of tricks. When he finds you not worrying in a situation where worry was possible, he tries to convince you that by beginning to worry you can 'do something' to avert the danger. Nine times out of ten this turns out on inspection to be bosh. On other days he becomes very moral: he says it is 'selfish' or 'complacent' of you to be feeling like that— although, at the very moment of his accusation, you may be setting out to render the only service in your power. If he has discovered a certain weak point in you, he will say you are being 'adolescent'; to which I always reply that he's getting terribly middle-aged.

But his favourite line, in these days, is to confuse the issue. He will pretend, if you let him, that the pleasure, say, in other people's domesticities is based on illusion. He will point out to you at great length (evidence never bothers him) that if you went into any one of those houses you would find every sort of skeleton in every cupboard. But he is only trying to muddle you. The pleasure involves, or need involve, no illusion at all. Distant hills look blue. They still look blue even after you have discovered that this particular beauty disappears when you approach them. The fact that they look blue fifteen miles away is just as much a fact as anything else. If we are to be realists, let us have realism all round. It is a mere brute fact that patches of that boyhood, remembered in one's forties at the bidding of some sudden smell or sound, give one (in the forties) an almost unbearable pleasure. The one is as good a fact as the other. Nothing would induce me to return to the age of fourteen: but neither would anything induce me to forgo the exquisite Proustian or Wordsworthian moments in which that part of the past sometimes returns to me.

We have had enough, once and for all, of Hedonism—the gloomy philosophy which says that Pleasure is the only good. But we have hardly yet begun what may be called *Hedonics*, the science or philosophy of Pleasure. And I submit that the first step in Hedonics is to knock the Jailer down and keep the keys henceforward in our own possession. He has dominated our minds for thirty years or so, and specially in the field of literature and literary criticism. He is a sham realist. He accuses all myth and fantasy and romance of wishful thinking: the way to silence him is to be more realist than he—to lay our ears closer to the murmur of life as it actually flows through us at every moment and to discover there all that quivering and wonder and (in a sense) infinity which the literature that he calls realistic omits. For the story which gives us the experience most like the experiences of living is not necessarily the story whose events are most like those in a biography or a newspaper.

XI

AFTER PRIGGERY — WHAT?

No doubt priggery is a horrid thing, and the more moral the horrider. To avoid a man's society because he is poor or ugly or stupid may be bad; but to avoid it because he is wicked — with the all but inevitable implication that you are less wicked (at least in some respect) — is dangerous and disgusting. We could all go on to develop this theme at any length and without the slightest effort. Smug — complacent — Pharisaical — Victorian — parable of the Pharisee and the Publican ... it writes itself. Upon my word, I have some difficulty in bridling the pen.

But the real question is what are we to put in the place of priggery. Private vices, we were taught long ago, are public benefits. Which means that when you remove a vice you must put a virtue in its place — a virtue which will produce the same public benefits. It will not do simply to cut out priggery and leave it at that.

These reflections arose out of the sort of conversation one often has. Suppose a man tells me that he has recently been lunching with a gentleman whom we will call Cleon. My informant is an honest man and a man of good will. Cleon is a wicked journalist, a man who disseminates for money falsehoods calculated to produce envy, hatred, suspicion, and confusion. At least that is what I believe Cleon to be; I have caught him lying myself. But it does not matter for purposes of the present argument whether my judgement of Cleon is correct or no. The point is that my honest friend fully agreed with it. The very reason why he mentioned the lunch party was that he wanted to tell me some more than usually foetid instance of Cleon's mendacity.

That, then, is the position we are in after the expulsion of priggery. My friend believes Cleon to be as false as hell; but he meets him on perfectly friendly terms over a lunch table. In a priggish or self-righteous society Cleon would occupy the same social status as a prostitute. His social contacts would extend only to clients, fellow-professionals, moral welfare-workers, and the police. Indeed, in a society which was rational as well as priggish (if such a combination could occur) his status would be a good deal lower than hers. The intellectual virginity which he has sold is a dearer treasure than her physical virginity. He gives his patrons a baser pleasure than she. He infects them with more dangerous diseases. Yet not one of us hesitates to eat with him, drink with him, joke with him, shake his hand, and, what is much worse, very few of us refrain from reading what he writes.

It will hardly be maintained that this complaisance springs from a sudden increase of our charity. We are not associating with Cleon as a friar or a clergyman from a mission or a member of the Salvation Army might associate with the prostitute. It is not our Christian love for the villain that has conquered our hatred of the villainy. We do not even pretend to love the villain; I have never in my life heard anyone speak well of him. As for the villainy, if we do not love it, we take it as a thing of course with a tolerant laugh or a shrug. We have lost the invaluable faculty of being shocked — a faculty which has hitherto almost distinguished the Man or Woman from the beast or the child. In a word, we have not risen above priggery; we have sunk below it.

The result is that things are a good deal too easy for Cleon. Even when the rewards of dishonesty are strictly alternative to those of honesty some men will choose them. But Cleon finds he can have both. He can enjoy all the sense of secret power and all the sweets of a perpetually gratified inferiority complex while at the same time having the *entrée* to honest society. From such conditions what can we expect but an increasing number of Cleons?

And that must be our ruin. If we remain a democracy they render impossible the formation of any healthy public opinion. If—*absit omen*—the totalitarian threat is realised, they will be the cruellest and dirtiest tools of government.

I submit, therefore, that the rest of us must really return to the old and 'priggish' habit of sending such people to Coventry.[1] And I am not quite convinced that we need to be prigs in doing so. The charge brought against us—Cleon himself will do it very well, possibly next week—will be that in cold-shouldering a man for his vices we are claiming to be better than he. This sounds very dreadful: but I wonder whether it may not be a turnip ghost?

If I meet a friend in the street who is drunk and pilot him home, I do, by the mere act of piloting him, imply that I am sober. If you press it this implies the claim that I am, for that one moment and in that one respect, 'better' than he. Mince it as you will, the mere brute fact is that I can walk straight and he can't. I am not saying in the least that I am in general a better man. Or again, in a lawsuit, I say I am in the right and the other man is in the wrong. I claim that particular superiority over him. It is really quite off the point to remind me that he has qualities of courage,

---

[1] i.e., to refuse to associate with them.

good-temper, unselfishness, and the like. It may well be so. I never denied it. But the question was about the title to a field or the damage done by a cow.

Now it seems to me that we can (and should) black-ball Cleon at every club and avoid his society and boycott his paper without in the least claiming any general superiority to him. We know perfectly well that he may be in the last resort a better man than we. We do not know by what stages he became the thing he is, nor how hard he may have struggled to be something better. Perhaps a bad heredity . . . unpopularity at school . . . complexes . . . a disgraceful record from the last war but one still nagging him on wakeful nights . . . a disastrous marriage. Who knows? Perhaps strong and sincere political convictions first bred intense desire that his side should prevail, and this first taught him to lie for what seemed a good cause and then, little by little, lying became his profession. God knows, we are not saying that we, placed as Cleon, would have done better. But for the moment, however it came about—and let us sing *non nobis* loud enough to lift the roof—we are not professional liars and he is. We may have a hundred vices from which he is free. But on one particular matter we are, if you insist, 'better' than he.

And that one thing which he does and we do not do is poisoning the whole nation. To prevent the poisoning is an urgent necessity. It cannot be prevented by the law: partly because we do not wish the law to have too much power over freedom of speech, and partly, perhaps, for another reason. The only safe way of silencing Cleon is by discrediting him. What cannot be done—and indeed ought not to be done—by law, can be done by public opinion. A 'sanitary cordon' can be drawn round Cleon. If no one but Cleon's like read his paper, much less meet him on terms of social intercourse, his trade will soon be reduced to harmless proportions.

To abstain from reading—and *a fortiori* from buying—a paper which you have once caught telling lies seems a very moderate form of asceticism. Yet how few practise it! Again and again I find people with Cleon's dirty sheets in their hands. They admit that he is a rogue but 'one must keep up with the times, must know what is being said'. That is one of the ways Cleon puts it across us. It is a fallacy. If we must find out what bad men are writing, and must therefore buy their papers, and therefore enable their papers to exist, who does not see that this supposed necessity of observing the evil is just what maintains the evil? It may in general be dangerous to ignore an evil; but not if the evil is one that perishes by being ignored.

But, you say, even if we ignore it others will not. Cleon's readers are not all the half-heartedly honest people whom I describe. Some of them are real rascals like Cleon himself. They are not interested in truth. That, no doubt, is so. But I am not convinced that the number of thoroughgoing rascals is large enough to keep Cleon afloat. In the present 'tolerant' age he has the support and countenance not only of the rascals but of thousands of honest people as well. Is it not at least worth our while to try the experiment of leaving him and the rascals alone? We might try it for five years. Let him for five years be sent to Coventry. I doubt if you will find him still rampant at the end. And why not begin today by countermanding your order for his paper?

XII

MODERN MAN AND HIS
CATEGORIES OF THOUGHT

Though we ought always to imitate the procedure of
Christ and His saints this pattern has to be adapted to the
changing conditions of history. We are not to preach in
Aramaic because the Baptist did so nor to recline at table
because the Lord reclined. One of the most difficult adap-
tations we have to make is in our methods of approaching
the unconverted.

The earliest missionaries, the Apostles, preached to
three sorts of men: to Jews, to those Judaising Gentiles
who were technically called *metuentes,* and to Pagans. In
all three classes they could count on certain predispositions which we cannot count on in our audience. All three
classes believed in the supernatural (even the Epicureans,
though they thought the gods inoperative). All were conscious of sin and feared divine judgement. Epicureanism,
by the very fact that it promised liberation from that fear,
proves its prevalence—a patent medicine can succeed only

by claiming to cure a widespread disease. The mystery religions offered purification and release and in all three classes most men believed that the world had once been better than it now was. The Jewish doctrine of the Fall, the Stoic conception of the Golden Age, and the common Pagan reverence for heroes, ancestors, and ancient lawgivers, were in this respect more or less agreed.

The world which we must try to convert shares none of those predispositions. In the last hundred years the public mind has been radically altered. In producing that alteration the following causes seem to me to have been at work.

(1) A revolution in the education of the most highly educated classes. This education was formerly based throughout Europe on the Ancients. If only the learned were Platonists or Aristotelians, the ordinary aristocrat was a Virgilian or, at the very least, a Horatian. Thus in Christian and sceptic alike there was a strong infusion of the better elements of Paganism. Even those who lacked piety had some sympathetic understanding of *pietàs.* It was natural to men so trained to believe that valuable truth could still be found in an ancient book. It was natural to them to reverence tradition. Values quite different from those of modern industrial civilisation were constantly present to their minds. Even where Christian belief was rejected there was still a standard against which contemporary ideals could

be judged. The effect of removing this education has been to isolate the mind in its own age; to give it, in relation to time, that disease which, in relation to space, we call Provincialism. The mere fact that St Paul wrote so long ago is, to a modern man, presumptive evidence against his having uttered important truths. The tactics of the enemy in this matter are simple and can be found in any military text-book. Before attacking a regiment you try, if you can, to *cut it off* from the regiments on each side.

(2) The Emancipation of Women. (I am not of course saying that this is a bad thing *in itself;* I am only considering one effect it has had in fact.) One of the determining factors in social life is that in general (there are numerous individual exceptions) men like men better than women like women. Hence, the freer women become, the fewer exclusively male assemblies there are. Most men, if free, retire frequently into the society of their own sex: women, if free, do this less often. In modern social life the sexes are more continuously mixed than they were in earlier periods. This probably has many good results: but it has one bad result. Among young people, obviously, it reduces the amount of serious argument about ideas. When the young male bird is in the presence of the young female it must (Nature insists) *display its plumage.* Any mixed society thus becomes the scene of wit, banter, persiflage,

anecdote—of everything in the world rather than prolonged and rigorous discussion on ultimate issues, or of
those serious masculine friendships in which such discussion arises. Hence, in our student population, a lower-
ing of metaphysical energy. The only serious questions
now discussed are those which seem to have a 'practical'
importance (i.e., the psychological and sociological prob-
lems), for these satisfy the intense practicality and con-
creteness of the female. That is, no doubt, her glory and
her proper contribution to the common wisdom of the
race. But the proper glory of the masculine mind, its disinterested concern with truth for truth's own sake, with
the cosmic and the metaphysical, is being impaired. Thus
again, as the previous change cuts us off from the past, this
cuts us off from the eternal. We are being further isolated;
forced down to the immediate and the quotidian.

(3) Developmentalism or Historicism. (I distinguish
sharply between the noble discipline called History and the
fatal pseudo-philosophy called Historicism.) The chief ori-
gin of this is Darwinianism. With Darwinianism as a theo-
rem in Biology I do not think a Christian need have any
quarrel. But what I call Developmentalism is the extension
of the evolutionary idea far beyond the biological realm: in
fact, its adoption as the key principle of reality. To the modern man it seems simply natural that an ordered cosmos

should emerge from chaos, that life should come out of the inanimate, reason out of instinct, civilisation out of savagery, virtue out of animalism. This idea is supported in his mind by a number of false analogies: the oak coming from the acorn, the man from the spermatozoon, the modern steamship from the primitive coracle. The supplementary truth that every acorn was dropped by an oak, every spermatozoon derived from a man, and the first boat by something so much more complex than itself as a man of genius, is simply ignored. The modern mind accepts as a formula for the universe in general the principle 'Almost nothing may be expected to turn into almost everything' without noticing that the parts of the universe under our direct observation tell a quite different story. This Developmentalism, in the field of human history, becomes Historicism: the belief that the scanty and haphazard selection of facts we know about History contains an almost mystical revelation of reality, and that to grasp the *Worden* and go wherever it is going is our prime duty. It will be seen that this view is not incompatible with all religion: indeed it goes very well with certain types of Pantheism. But it is wholly inimical to Christianity, for it denies both creation and the Fall. Where, for Christianity, the Best creates the good and the good is corrupted by sin, for Developmentalism the very standard of good is itself in a state of flux.

(4) What we may call Proletarianism, in its various forms ranging from strict Marxism to vague 'democracy'. A strong anti-clericalism has of course been a feature of continental Proletarianism almost from its beginnings. This element is generally said (and, I think, correctly) to be less present in the English forms. But what is common to all forms of it is the fact that the Proletariat in all countries (even those with 'Right' governments) has been consistently flattered for a great many years. The natural result has now followed. They are self-satisfied to a degree perhaps beyond the self-satisfaction of any recorded aristocracy. They are convinced that whatever may be wrong with the world it cannot be themselves. Someone else must be to blame for every evil. Hence, when the existence of God is discussed, they by no means think of Him as their Judge. On the contrary, they are His judges. If He puts up a reasonable defence they will consider it and perhaps acquit Him. They have no feelings of fear, guilt, or awe. They think, from the very outset, of God's duties to them, not their duties to Him. And God's duties to them are conceived not in terms of salvation but in purely secular terms—social security, prevention of war, a higher standard of life. 'Religion' is judged exclusively by its contribution to these ends. This overlaps with the next heading.

(5) Practicality. Man is becoming as narrowly 'practical' as the irrational animals. In lecturing to popular audiences I have repeatedly found it almost impossible to make them understand that I recommended Christianity because I thought its affirmations to be objectively *true.* They are simply not interested in the question of truth or falsehood. They only want to know if it will be comforting, or 'inspiring', or socially useful. (In English we have a peculiar difficulty here because in popular speech 'believe in' has two meanings, (a) To accept as true, (b) To approve of—e.g., 'I believe in free trade'. Hence when an Englishman says he 'believes in' or 'does not believe in' Christianity, he may not be thinking about *truth* at all. Very often he is only telling us whether he approves or disapproves of the Church as a social institution.) Closely connected with this unhuman Practicality is an indifference to, and contempt of, dogma. The popular point of view is unconsciously syncretistic: it is widely believed that 'all religions really mean the same thing'.

(6) Scepticism about Reason. Practicality, combined with vague notions of what Freud, or Einstein, said, has produced a general, and quite *unalarmed,* belief that reasoning proves nothing and that all thought is conditioned by irrational processes. More than once in argument with an intelligent man (*not* a member of the Intelligentsia) I

have pointed out that the position he took up would logically involve a denial of the validity of thought, and he has understood, and agreed with me, but has not regarded this as any objection to his original position. He accepts without dismay the conclusion that all our thoughts are invalid.

Such, in my opinion, are the main characteristics of the mental climate in which a modern evangelist has to work. One way of summarising it would be to say that I sometimes wonder whether we shall not have to re-convert men to real Paganism as a preliminary to converting them to Christianity. If they were Stoics, Orphics, Mithraists, or (better still) peasants worshipping the Earth, our task might be easier. That is why I do not regard contemporary Paganisms (Theosophy, Anthroposophy, etc.) as a wholly bad symptom.

There are, of course, also good elements in the present situation. There is, perhaps, more social conscience than there has ever been before: and though chastity in conduct is probably low I think modern young people are perhaps less prurient and less obsessed with lascivious thought than more modest and decorous ages have been. (This is only an impression, and may be mistaken.) I also think that the very fact of our isolation, the fact that we are coming to be almost the only people who appeal to the buried (but not dead) human appetite for the objective truth, may be a source of strength as well as of difficulty. Before closing, I must add that the limitation of my own gifts has compelled me always to use a predominantly intellectual approach. But I have also been present when an appeal of a much more emotional and also more 'pneumatic', kind has worked wonders on a modern audience. Where God gives the gift, the 'foolishness of preaching'[1] is still mighty. But best of all is a team of two: one to deliver the preliminary intellectual barrage, and the other to follow up with a direct attack on the heart.

---

[1] 1 Corinthians 1:21.

XIII

TALKING ABOUT BICYCLES

'Talking about bicycles,' said my friend, 'I have been through the four ages. I can remember a time in early childhood when a bicycle meant nothing to me: it was just part of the huge, meaningless background of grown-up gadgets against which life went on. Then came a time when to have a bicycle, and to have learned to ride it, and to be at last spinning along on one's own, early in the morning, under trees, in and out of the shadows, was like entering Paradise. That apparently effortless and friction-less gliding—more like swimming than any other motion, but really most like the discovery of a fifth element—that seemed to have solved the secret of life. Now one would begin to be happy. But, of course, I soon reached the third period. Pedalling to and fro from school (it was one of those journeys that feel up-hill both ways) in all weathers, soon revealed the prose of cycling. The bicycle, itself, be-came to me what his oar is to a galley slave.'

'But what was the fourth age?' I asked.

'I am in it now, or rather I am frequently in it. I have had to go back to cycling lately now that there's no car. And the jobs I use it for are often dull enough. But again and again the mere fact of riding brings back a delicious whiff of memory. I recover the feelings of the second age. What's more, I see how true they were—how philosophical, even. For it really is a remarkably pleasant motion. To be sure, it is not a recipe for happiness as I then thought. In that sense the second age was a mirage. But a mirage of something.'

'How do you mean?' said I.

'I mean this. Whether there is, or whether there is not, in this world or in any other, the kind of happiness which one's first experiences of cycling seemed to promise, still, on any view, it is something to have had the idea of it. The value of the thing promised remains even if that particular promise was false—even if all possible promises of it are false.'

'Sounds like a carrot in front of a donkey's nose,' said I.

'Even that wouldn't be quite a cheat if the donkey enjoyed the smell of carrots as much as, or more than, the taste. Or suppose the smell raised in the donkey emotions which no actual eating could ever satisfy? Wouldn't he look back (when he was an old donkey, living in the fourth age) and say, "I'm glad I had that carrot tied in front of my nose. Otherwise I might still have thought eating was the greatest happiness. Now I know there's something far better—the something that came to me in the smell of the carrot. And I'd rather have known that—even if I'm never to get it—than not to have known it, for even to have wanted it is what makes life worth having."'

'I don't think a donkey would feel like that at all.'

'No. Neither a four-legged donkey nor a two-legged one. But I have a suspicion that to feel that way is the real mark of a human.'

'So that no one was human till bicycles were invented?'

'The bicycle is only one instance. I think there are these four ages about nearly everything. Let's give them names. They are the Unenchanted Age, the Enchanted Age, the Disenchanted Age, and the Re-enchanted Age. As a little child I was Unenchanted about bicycles. Then, when I first learned to ride, I was Enchanted. By sixteen I was Disenchanted and now I am Re-enchanted.'

'Go on,' said I. 'What are some of the other applications?'

'I suppose the most obvious is love. We all remember the Unenchanted Age—there was a time when women meant nothing to us. Then we fell in love; that, of course, was the Enchantment. Then, in the early or middle years of marriage there came—well, Disenchantment. All the promises had turned out, in a way, false. No woman could be expected—the thing was impossible—I don't mean any disrespect either to my own wife or to yours. But—'

'I was never married,' I reminded him.

'Oh! That's a pity. For in that case you can't possibly understand this particular form of Re-enchantment. I don't think I could explain to a bachelor how there comes a time when you look back on that first mirage, perfectly well aware that it was a mirage, and yet, seeing all the things that have come out of it, things the boy and girl could never have dreamed of, and feeling also that to remember it is, in a sense, to bring it back in reality, so that under all the other experiences it is still there like a shell lying at the bottom of a clear, deep pool—and that nothing would have happened at all without it—so that even where it was least true it was telling you important truths in the only form you would then understand—but I see I'm boring you.'

'Not at all,' said I.

'Let's take an example that may interest you more. How about war? Most of our juniors were brought up Unenchanted about war. The Unenchanted man sees (quite correctly) the waste and cruelty and sees nothing else. The Enchanted man is in the Rupert Brooke or Philip Sidney state of mind—he's thinking of glory and battle-poetry and forlorn hopes and last stands and chivalry. Then comes the Disenchanted Age—say Siegfried Sassoon. But there is also a fourth stage, though very few people in modern England dare to talk about it. You know quite well what I mean. One is not in the least deceived: we remember the trenches too well. We know how much of the reality the romantic view left out. But we also know that heroism is a real thing, that all the plumes and flags and trumpets of the tradition were not there for nothing. They were an attempt to honour what is truly honourable: what was first perceived to be honourable precisely because everyone knew how horrible war is. And that's where this business of the Fourth Age is so important.'

'How do you mean?'

'Isn't it immensely important to distinguish Unenchantment from Disenchantment—and Enchantment from Re-enchantment? In the poets, for instance. The war poetry of Homer or *The Battle of Maldon,* for example, is Re-enchantment. You see in every line that the poet knows, quite as well as any modern, the horrible thing he is writing about. He celebrates heroism but he has paid the proper price for doing so. He sees the horror and yet sees also the glory. In the *Lays of Ancient Rome,* on the other hand, or in *Lepanto* (jolly as *Lepanto* is) one is still enchanted: the poets obviously have no idea what a battle is like.[1] Similarly with Unenchantment and Disenchantment. You read an author in whom love is treated as lust and all war as murder—and so forth. But are you reading a Disenchanted man or only an Unenchanted man? Has the writer been through the Enchantment and come out on to the bleak highlands, or is he simply a subman who is free from the love mirage as a dog is free, and free from the heroic mirage as a coward is free? If Disenchanted, he may have something worth hearing to say, though less than a Re-enchanted man. If Unenchanted, into the fire with his book. He is talking of what he doesn't understand. But the great danger we have to guard against in this age is the Unenchanted man, mistaking himself for, and mistaken by others for, the Disenchanted man. What were you going to say?'

'I was just wondering whether the Enchantment which you claim to look back on from the final stage was often no more than an illusion of memory. Doesn't one remember a good many more exciting experiences than one has really had?'

---

[1] *The Battle of Maldon,* a poem in Old English of the tenth century, is about the raid of the Northmen under Anlaf, at Maldon in Essex, in 991. The *Lays of Ancient Rome* (1842) are by Thomas Macaulay, and *Lepanto* (1911) is by G. K. Chesterton.

'Why yes. In a sense. Memory itself is the supreme example of the four ages. Wordsworth, you see, was Enchanted. He got delicious gleams of memory from his early youth and took them at their face value. He believed that if he could have got back to certain spots in his own past he would find there the moment of joy waiting for him. You are Disenchanted. You've begun to suspect that those moments, of which the memory is now so ravishing, weren't at the time quite so wonderful as they now seem. You're right. They weren't. Each great experience is

a whisper
Which Memory will warehouse as a shout.[2]

But what then? Isn't the warehousing just as much a fact as anything else? Is the vision any less important because a particular kind of polarised light between past and present happens to be the mechanism that brings it into focus? Isn't it a fact about mountains—as good a fact as any other—that they look purple at a certain distance?—If you won't have any more beer perhaps we'd better be getting along. That man on the other side of the bar thinks we've been talking politics.'

---

[2] From an unpublished poem by Owen Barfield.

'I'm not sure that we haven't,' said I.

'You're quite right. You mean that Aristocracy is one other example? It was the merest Enchantment to suppose that any human beings, trusted with uncontrolled powers over their fellows, would not use it for exploitation; or even to suppose that their own standards of honour, valour, and elegance (for which alone they existed) would not soon degenerate into flash-vulgarity. Hence, rightly and inevitably, the Disenchantment, the age of Revolutions. But the question on which all hangs is whether we can go on to Re-enchantment.'

'What would that Re-enchantment be?'

'The realisation that the thing of which Aristocracy was a mirage is a vital necessity; if you like, that Aristocracy was right: it was only the Aristocrats who were wrong. Or, putting it the other way, that a society which becomes democratic in *ethos* as well as in constitution is doomed. And not much loss either.'

XIV

ON LIVING IN AN ATOMIC AGE

In one way we think a great deal too much of the atomic bomb. 'How are we to live in an atomic age?' I am tempted to reply: 'Why, as you would have lived in the sixteenth century when the plague visited London almost every year, or as you would have lived in a Viking age when raiders from Scandinavia might land and cut your throat any night; or indeed, as you are already living in an age of cancer, an age of syphilis, an age of paralysis, an age of air raids, an age of railway accidents, an age of motor accidents.'

In other words, do not let us begin by exaggerating the novelty of our situation. Believe me, dear sir or madam, you and all whom you love were already sentenced to death before the atomic bomb was invented: and quite a high percentage of us were going to die in unpleasant ways. We had, indeed, one very great advantage over our ancestors—anaesthetics; but we have that still. It is perfectly ridiculous to go about whimpering and drawing long faces because the scientists have added one more chance of painful and premature death to a world which already bristled with such chances and in which death itself was not a chance at all, but a certainty.

This is the first point to be made: and the first action to be taken is to pull ourselves together. If we are all going to be destroyed by an atomic bomb, let that bomb when it comes find us doing sensible and human things—praying, working, teaching, reading, listening to music, bathing the children, playing tennis, chatting to our friends over a pint and a game of darts—not huddled together like frightened sheep and thinking about bombs. They may break our bodies (a microbe can do that) but they need not dominate our minds.

'But,' you reply, 'it is not death—not even painful and premature death—that we are bothering about. Of course the chance of *that* is not new. What is new is that the atomic bomb may finally and totally destroy civilisation itself. The lights may be put out for ever.'

This brings us much nearer to the real point; but let me try to make clear exactly what I think that point is. What were your views about the ultimate future of civilisation *before* the atomic bomb appeared on the scene? What did you think all this effort of humanity was to come to in the end? The real answer is known to almost everyone who has even a smattering of science; yet, oddly enough, it is hardly ever mentioned. And the real answer (almost beyond doubt) is that, with or without atomic bombs, the whole story is going to end in NOTHING. The astronomers hold out no hope that this planet is going to be permanently inhabitable. The physicists hold out no hope that organic life is going to be a permanent possibility in any part of the material universe. Not only this earth, but the whole show, all the suns of space, are to run down. Nature is a sinking ship. Bergson talks about the *élan vital,* and Mr Shaw talks about the 'Life-force' as if they could surge on for ever and ever. But that comes of concentrating on biology and ignoring the other sciences. There is really no such hope. Nature does not, in the long run, favour life. If Nature is all that exists—in other words, if there is no God and no life of some quite different sort somewhere outside Nature—then all stories will end in the same way: in a universe from which all life is banished without possibility of return. It will have been an accidental flicker, and there will be no one even to remember it. No doubt atomic bombs may cut its duration on this present planet shorter that it might have been; but the whole thing, even if it lasted for billions of years, must be so infinitesimally short in relation to the oceans of dead time which precede and follow it that I cannot feel excited about its curtailment.

What the wars and the weather (are we in for another of those periodic ice ages?) and the atomic bomb have really done is to remind us forcibly of the sort of world we are living in and which, during the prosperous period before 1914, we were beginning to forget. And this reminder is, so far as it goes, a good thing. We have been waked from a pretty dream, and now we can begin to talk about realities.

We see at once (when we have been waked) that the important question is not whether an atomic bomb is going to obliterate 'civilisation'. The important question is whether 'Nature'—the thing studied by the sciences—is the only thing in existence. Because if you answer *yes* to the second question, then the first question only amounts to asking whether the inevitable frustration of all human activities may be hurried on by our own action instead of coming at its natural time. That is, of course, a question that concerns us very much. Even on a ship which will certainly sink sooner or later, the news that the boiler might blow up *now* would not be heard with indifference by anyone. But those who knew that the ship was sinking in any case would not, I think, be quite so desperately excited as those who had forgotten this fact, and were vaguely imagining that it might arrive somewhere.

It is, then, on the second question that we really need to make up our minds. And let us begin by supposing that Nature is all that exists. Let us suppose that nothing ever has existed or ever will exist except this meaningless play of atoms in space and time: that by a series of hundredth chances it has (regrettably) produced things like ourselves—conscious beings who now know that their own consciousness is an accidental result of the whole meaningless process and is therefore itself meaningless, though to us (alas!) it *feels* significant.

In this situation there are, I think, three things one might do:

(1) You might commit suicide. Nature which has (blindly, accidentally) given me for my torment this consciousness which demands meaning and value in a universe that offers neither, has luckily also given me the means of getting rid of it. I return the unwelcome gift. I will be fooled no longer.

(2) You might decide simply to have as good a time as possible. The universe is a universe of nonsense, but since you are here, grab what you can. Unfortunately, however, there is, on these terms, so very little left to grab—only the coarsest sensual pleasures. You can't, except in the lowest animal sense, be in love with a girl if you know (and keep on remembering) that all the beauties both of her person

and of her character are a momentary and accidental pattern produced by the collision of atoms, and that your own response to them is only a sort of psychic phosphorescence arising from the behaviour of your genes. You can't go on getting any very serious pleasure from music if you know and remember that its air of significance is a pure illusion, that you like it only because your nervous system is irrationally conditioned to like it. You may still, in the lowest sense, have a 'good time'; but just in so far as it becomes very good, just in so far as it ever threatens to push you on from cold sensuality into real warmth and enthusiasm and joy, so far you will be forced to feel the hopeless disharmony between your own emotions and the universe in which you really live.

(3) You may defy the universe. You may say, 'Let it be irrational, I am not. Let it be merciless, I will have mercy. By whatever curious chance it has produced me, now that I am here I will live according to human values. I know the universe will win in the end, but what is that to me? I will go down fighting. Amid all this wastefulness I will persevere; amid all this competition, I will make sacrifices. Be damned to the universe!'

I suppose that most of us, in fact, while we remain materialists, adopt a more or less uneasy alternation between the second and the third attitude. And although the third is incomparably the better (it is, for instance, much more likely to 'preserve civilisation'), both really shipwreck on the same rock. That rock—the disharmony between our own hearts and Nature—is obvious in the second. The third seems to avoid the rock by accepting disharmony from the outset and defying it. But it will not really work. In it, you hold up our own human standards against the idiocy of the universe. That is, we talk as if our own standards were something *outside* the universe which can be contrasted with it; as if we could judge the universe by some standard borrowed *from another source*. But if (as we were supposing) Nature—the space-time-matter system—is the only thing in existence, then of course there can be no other source for our standards. They must, like everything else, be the unintended and meaningless outcome of blind forces. Far from being a light from beyond Nature whereby Nature can be judged, they are only the way in which anthropoids of our species feel when the atoms under our own skulls get into certain states—those states being produced by causes quite irrational, unhuman, and non-moral. Thus the very ground on which we defy Nature crumbles under our feet. The standard we are applying is tainted at the source. If our standards are derived from this meaningless universe they must be as meaningless as it.

For most modern people, I think, thoughts of this kind have to be gone through before the opposite view can get a fair hearing. All Naturalism leads us to this in the end—to a quite final and hopeless discord between what our minds claim to be and what they really must be if Naturalism is true. They claim to be spirit; that is, to be reason, perceiving universal intellectual principles and universal moral laws and possessing free will. But if Naturalism is true they must in reality be merely arrangements of atoms in skulls, coming about by irrational causation. We never think a thought because it is true, only because blind Nature forces us to think it. We never do an act because it is right, only because blind Nature forces us to do it. It is when one has faced this preposterous conclusion that one is at last ready to listen to the voice that whispers: 'But suppose we really are spirits? Suppose we are not the offspring of Nature ... ?'

For, really, the naturalistic conclusion is unbelievable. For one thing, it is only through trusting our own minds that we have come to know Nature herself. If Nature when fully known seems to teach us (that is, if the sciences teach us) that our own minds are chance arrangements of atoms, then there must have been some mistake; for if that were so, then the sciences themselves would be chance arrangements of atoms and we should have no reason for believing in them. There is only one way to avoid this deadlock. We must go back to a much earlier view. We must simply accept it that we are spirits, free and rational beings, at present inhabiting an irrational universe, and must draw the conclusion that we are *not derived from it.* We are strangers here. We come from somewhere else. Nature is not the only thing that exists. There is 'another world', and that is where we come from. And that explains why we do not feel at home here. A fish feels at home in the water. If we 'belonged here' we should feel at home here. All that we say about 'Nature red in tooth and claw', about death and time and mutability, all our half-amused, half-bashful attitude to our own bodies, is quite inexplicable on the theory that we are simply natural creatures. If this world is the only world, how did we come to find its laws either so dreadful or so comic? If there is no straight line elsewhere, how did we discover that Nature's line is crooked?

But what, then, is Nature, and how do we come to be imprisoned in a system so alien to us? Oddly enough, the question becomes much less sinister the moment one realises that Nature is not all. Mistaken for our mother, she is terrifying and even abominable. But if she is only our sister—if she and we have a common Creator—if she is our sparring partner—then the situation is quite tolerable. Perhaps we are not here as prisoners but as colonists: only consider what we have done already to the dog, the horse, or the daffodil. She is indeed a rough playfellow. There are elements of evil in her. To explain that would carry us far back: I should have to speak of Powers and Principalities and all that would seem to a modern reader most mythological. This is not the place, nor do these questions come first. It is enough to say here that Nature, like us but in her different way, is much alienated from her Creator, though in her, as in us, gleams of the old beauty remain. But they are there not to be worshipped but to be enjoyed. She has nothing to teach us. It is our business to live by our own law not by hers: to follow, in private or in public life, the law of love and temperance even when they seem to be suicidal, and not the law of competition and grab, even when they seem to be necessary to our survival. For it is part of our spiritual law never to put survival first: not even the survival of our species. We must resolutely train ourselves to feel that the survival of Man on this Earth, much more of our own nation or culture or class, is not worth having unless it can be had by honourable and merciful means.

The sacrifice is not so great as it seems. Nothing is more likely to destroy a species or a nation than a determination to survive at all costs. Those who care for something else more than civilisation are the only people by whom civilisation is at all likely to be preserved. Those who want Heaven most have served Earth best. Those who love Man less than God do most for Man.

XV

THE EMPTY UNIVERSE[1]

This book is, I believe, the first attempt to reverse a movement of thought which has been going on since the beginning of philosophy.

The process whereby man has come to know the universe is from one point of view extremely complicated; from another it is alarmingly simple. We can observe a single one-way progression. At the outset the universe appears packed with will, intelligence, life, and positive qualities; every tree is a nymph and every planet a god. Man himself is akin to the gods. The advance of knowledge gradually empties this rich and genial universe: first of its gods, then of its colours, smells, sounds, and tastes, finally of solidity itself as solidity was originally imagined. As these items are taken from the world, they are transferred to the subjective side of the account: classi-

---

[1] This essay was first published as a Preface to D. E. Harding's *The Hierarchy of Heaven and Earth: A New Diagram of Man in the Universe* (London, 1952).

fied as our sensations, thoughts, images, or emotions. The Subject becomes gorged, inflated, at the expense of the Object. But the matter does not rest there. The same method which has emptied the world now proceeds to empty ourselves. The masters of the method soon announce that we were just as mistaken (and mistaken in much the same way) when we attributed 'souls', or 'selves' or 'minds' to human organisms, as when we attributed Dryads to the trees. Animism, apparently, begins at home. We, who have personified all other things, turn out to be ourselves mere personifications. Man is indeed akin to the gods: that is, he is no less phantasmal than they. Just as the Dryad is a 'ghost', an abbreviated symbol for all the facts we know about the tree foolishly mistaken for a mysterious entity over and above the facts, so the man's 'mind' or 'consciousness' is an abbreviated symbol for certain verifiable facts about his behaviour: a symbol mistaken for a thing. And just as we have been broken of our bad habit of personifying trees, so we must now be broken of our bad habit of personifying men: a reform already effected in the political field. There never was a Subjective account into which we could transfer the items which the Object had lost. There is no 'consciousness' to contain, as images or private experiences, all the lost gods, colours, and concepts.

Consciousness is 'not the sort of noun that can be used that way'.

For we are given to understand that our mistake was a linguistic one. All our previous theologies, metaphysics, and psychologies were a by-product of our bad grammar. Max Müller's formula (Mythology is a disease of language)[2] thus returns with a wider scope than he ever dreamed of. We were not even imagining these things, we were only talking confusedly. All the questions which humanity has hitherto asked with deepest concern for the answer turn out to be unanswerable; not because the answers are hidden from us like 'goddes privitee',[3] but because they are nonsense questions like 'How far is it from London Bridge to Christmas Day?' What we thought we were loving when we loved a woman or a friend was not even a phantom like the phantom sail which starving sailors think they see on the horizon. It was something more like a pun or a *sophisma per figuram dictionis*.[4] It is as though a man, deceived by the linguistic similarity between 'myself' and 'my spectacles', should start looking round for his 'self' to put in his pocket

---

[2] Friedrich Max Müller, *The Science of Language* (1864), Second Series, Lecture viii on 'Metaphor'.
[3] Geoffrey Chaucer, *The Canterbury Tales*, The Miller's Prologue, line 3164.
[4] 'Sophism disguised as language.'

before he left his bedroom in the morning: he might want it during the course of the day. If we lament the discovery that our friends have no 'selves' in the old sense, we shall be behaving like a man who shed bitter tears at being unable to find his 'self' anywhere on the dressing-table or even underneath it.

And thus we arrive at a result uncommonly like zero. While we were reducing the world to almost nothing we deceived ourselves with the fancy that all its lost qualities were being kept safe (if in a somewhat humbled condition) as 'things in our own mind'. Apparently we had no mind of the sort required. The Subject is as empty as the Object. Almost nobody has been making linguistic mistakes about almost nothing. By and large, this is the only thing that has ever happened.

Now the trouble about this conclusion is not simply that it is unwelcome to our emotions. It is not unwelcome to them at all times or in all people. This philosophy, like every other, has its pleasures. And it will, I fancy, prove very congenial to government. The old 'liberty-talk' was very much mixed up with the idea that, as inside the ruler, so inside the subject, there was a whole world, to him the centre of all worlds, capacious of endless suffering and delight. But now, of course, he has no 'inside', except the sort you can find by cutting him open. If I had to burn a man alive, I think I should find this doctrine comfortable. The real difficulty for most of us is more like a physical difficulty: we find it impossible to keep our minds, even for ten seconds at a stretch, twisted into the shape that this philosophy demands. And, to do him justice, Hume (who is its great ancestor) warned us not to try. He recommended backgammon instead; and freely admitted that when, after a suitable dose, we returned to our theory, we should find it 'cold and strained and ridiculous'.[5] And obviously, if we really must accept nihilism, that is how we shall have to live: just as, if we have diabetes, we must take insulin. But one would rather not have diabetes and do without the insulin. If there should, after all, turn out to be any alternative to a philosophy that can be supported only by repeated (and presumably increasing) doses of backgammon, I suppose that most people would be glad to hear of it.

There is indeed (or so I am told) one way of living under this philosophy without the backgammon, but it is not one a man would like to try. I have heard that there are states of insanity in which such a nihilistic doctrine becomes really credible: that is, as Dr I. A. Richards would

---

[5] David Hume, *A Treatise of Human Nature* (1739–40), Book I, Part iv, section vii.

say, 'belief feelings' are attached to it.[6] The patient has the experience of being nobody in a world of nobodies and nothings. Those who return from this condition describe it as highly disagreeable.

Now there is of course nothing new in the attempt to arrest the process that has led us from the living universe where man meets the gods to the final void where almost-nobody discovers his mistakes about almost-nothing. Every step in that process has been contested. Many rear-guard actions have been fought: some are being fought at the moment. But it has only been a question of arresting, not of reversing, the movement. That is what makes Mr Harding's book so important. If it 'works', then we shall have seen the beginning of a reversal: not a stand here, or a stand there, but a kind of thought which attempts to reopen the whole question. And we feel sure in advance that only thought of this type can help. The fatal slip which has led us to nihilism must have occurred at the very beginning.

There is of course no question of returning to Animism as Animism was before the 'rot' began. No one supposes that the beliefs of pre-philosophic humanity, just as they stood before they were criticised, can or should

---

[6] I. A. Richards, *Principles of Literary Criticism* (1924), chapter XXXV.

be restored. The question is whether the first thinkers in modifying (and rightly modifying) them under the criticism, did not make some rash and unnecessary concession. It was certainly not their intention to commit us to the absurd consequences that have actually followed. This sort of error is of course very common in debate or even in our solitary thought. We start with a view which contains a good deal of truth, though in a confused or exaggerated form. Objections are then suggested and we withdraw it. But hours later we discover that we have emptied the baby out with the bath water and that the original view must have contained certain truths for lack of which we are now entangled in absurdities. So here. In emptying out the dryads and the gods (which, admittedly, 'would not do' just as they stood) we appear to have thrown out the whole universe, ourselves included. We must go back and begin over again: this time with a better chance of success, for of course we can now use all particular truths and all improvements of method which our argument may have thrown up as by-products in its otherwise ruinous course.

It would be affectation to pretend that I know whether Mr Harding's attempt, in its present form, will work. Very possibly not. One hardly expects the first, or the twenty-first, rocket to the Moon to make a good landing.

But it is a beginning. If it should turn out to have been even the remote ancestor of some system which will give us again a credible universe inhabited by credible agents and observers, this will still have been a very important book indeed.

It has also given me that bracing and satisfying experience which, in certain books of theory, seems to be partially independent of our final agreement or disagreement. It is an experience most easily disengaged by remembering what has happened to us whenever we turned from the inferior exponents of a system, even a system we reject, to its great doctors. I have had it on turning from common 'Existentialists' to M. Sartre himself, from Calvinists to the *Institutio,* from 'Transcendentalists' to Emerson, from books about 'Renaissance Platonism' to Ficino. One may still disagree (I disagree heartily with all the authors I have just named) but one now sees for the first time why anyone ever did agree. One has breathed a new air, become free of a new country. It may be a country you cannot live in, but you now know why the natives love it. You will henceforward see all systems a little differently because you have been inside that one. From this point of view philosophies have some of the same qualities as works of art. I am not referring at all to the literary art with which they may or may not be expressed. It is the *ipseitas,* the peculiar unity of effect produced by a special balancing and patterning of thoughts and classes of thoughts: a delight very like that which would be given by Hesse's *Glasperlenspiel* (in the book of that name) if it could really exist.[7] I owe a new experience of that kind to Mr Harding.

---

[7] Hermann Hesse's *Das Glasperlenspiel* (1943) has been translated into English as *The Glass Bead Game* by R. and C. Winston (London, 1970).

XVI

PRUDERY AND PHILOLOGY

We have had a good deal of discussion lately about what is called obscenity in literature, and this discussion has (very naturally) dealt with it chiefly from a legal or moral point of view. But the subject also gives rise to a specifically literary problem.

There have been very few societies, though there have been some, in which it was considered shameful to make a drawing of the naked human body: a detailed, unexpurgated drawing which omits nothing that the eye can see. On the other hand, there have been very few societies in which it would have been permissible to give an equally detailed description of the same subject in words. What is the cause of this seemingly arbitrary discrimination?

Before attempting to answer that question, let us note that the mere existence of the discrimination disposes of one widely accepted error. It proves that the objection to much that is called 'obscenity' in literature is not exclusively moral. If it were, if the objectors were con-

cerned merely to forbid what is likely to inflame appetite, the depicted nude should be as widely prohibited as
the described nude. It might, indeed, be regarded as the
more objectionable: *segnius irritant,* things seen move
men more than things reported. No doubt, some books,
and some pictures, have been censured on purely moral
grounds, censured as 'inflammatory'. But I am not speaking of such special cases: I am speaking of the quite general concession to the artist of that which is denied to the
writer. Something other than a care for chastity seems to
be involved.

And fortunately there is a very easy way of finding out
why the distinction exists. It is by experiment. Sit down
and draw your nude. When you have finished it, take your
pen and attempt the written description. Before you have
finished you will be faced with a problem which simply
did not exist while you were working at the picture. When
you come to those parts of the body which are not usually
mentioned, you will have to make a choice of vocabulary.
And you will find that you have only four alternatives: a
nursery word, an archaism, a word from the gutter, or a
scientific word. You will not find any ordinary, neutral
word, comparable to 'hand' or 'nose'. And this is going
to be very troublesome. Whichever of the four words you
choose is going to give a particular tone to your composi-

tion: willy-nilly you must produce baby-talk, or Wardour Street, or coarseness, or technical jargon. And each of these will force you to imply a particular attitude (which is not what you intended to imply) towards your material. The words will force you to write as if you thought it either childish, or quaint, or contemptible, or of purely scientific interest. In fact, *mere* description is impossible. Language forces you to an implicit comment. In the drawing you did not need to comment: you left the lines to speak for themselves. I am talking, of course, about mere draughtsmanship at its simplest level. A completed work by a real artist will certainly contain a comment about something. The point is that, when we use words instead of lines, there is really nothing that corresponds to mere draughtsmanship. The pen always does both less and more than the pencil.

This, by the by, is the most important of all facts about literature. There never was a falser maxim than *ut pictura poesis.* We are sometimes told that everything in the word can come into literature. This is perhaps true in some sense. But it is a dangerous truth unless we balance it with the statement that nothing can go into literature except words, or (if you prefer) that nothing can go in except by becoming words. And words, like every other medium, have their own proper powers and limitations. (They are, for instance, all but impotent when it comes to describing even the simplest machines. Who could, in words, explain what a screw, or a pair of scissors, is like?)

One of these limitations is that the common names (as distinct from the childish, archaic, or scientific names) for certain things are 'obscene' words. It is the words, not the things, that are obscene. That is, they are words long consecrated (or desecrated) to insult, derision, and buffoonery. You cannot use them without bringing in the whole atmosphere of the slum, the barrack-room, and the public school.

It may of course be said that this state of affairs—this lack of any neutral and straightforward words for certain things—is itself the result of precious prudery. Not, to be sure, of 'Victorian' or 'Puritan' prudery, as the ignorant say, but of a prudery certainly pre-Christian and probably primeval. (Quintilian on the 'indecencies' which his contemporaries found in Virgil is an eye-opener; no Victorian was ever so pruriently proper.) The modern writer, if he wishes to introduce into serious writing (comic works are a different matter) a total liberty for the pen such as has nearly always been allowed to the pencil, is in fact taking on a much more formidable adversary than a local (and, we may hope, temporary) state of English law. He is attempting to rip up the whole fabric of the mind. I do not say that success is impossible, still less that the attempt is perverse. But before we commit ourselves to so gigantic an enterprise, two questions seem to be worth asking.

First, is it worth it? Have good writers not better things to do? For of course the present state of the law, and (what is less easily utterable) of taste, cannot really prevent any writer worth his salt from saying, in effect, whatever he wants to say. I should insult the technical proficiency of our contemporaries if I supposed them so little masters of the medium as to be unable, whatever their theme, to evade the law. Many perhaps would feel such evasion to be disgraceful. Yet why? The contemporary state of sensibility is surely, like the language, part of the author's raw material. Evasion (I admit the word has a shabby sound) need not really be less creditable than the 'turning' of any other difficulty which one's medium presents. Great work can be done in a difficult metre; why not also under difficult restraints of another kind? When authors rail too much (we may allow them to rail a little) against public taste, do they perhaps betray some insufficiency? They denigrate what they ought rather to use and finally transform by first obeying.

Secondly, do we not stand to lose more than we gain? For of course to remove all 'prudery' is to remove one area of vivid sensibility, to expunge a human feeling. There are quite enough etiolated, inert, neutral words knocking about already: do we want to increase their number? A strict moralist might possibly argue that the old human reticence about some of our bodily functions has bred such mystery and prurience ('It is impossible', said the girl in Shaw, 'to explain decency without being indecent') that it cannot be abolished too soon. But would the strict moralist be right? Has nothing good come out of it? It is the parent of three-quarters of the world's jokes. Remove the standard of decency in the written word, and one of two results must follow. Either you can never laugh again at most of Aristophanes, Chaucer, or Rabelais, the joke having partly depended on the fact that what is mentioned is unmentionable, or, horrid thought, the oral *fableau* as we have all heard it in taproom (not by any means always vile or prurient, but often full of true humour and traditional art) will be replaced and killed by written, professional *fableaux:* just as the parlour games we played for ourselves fifty years ago are now played for us by professionals 'on the air'. The smoking-room story is, I grant, the last and least of the folk-arts. But it is the only one we have left. Should not writers be willing to preserve it at the cost of a slight restraint on their own vocabulary?

XVII

INTERIM REPORT

[This was the first of a series of articles in *The Cambridge Review* comparing Oxford and Cambridge, by authors who had seen something of both universities. From 1925 to 1954 Lewis had been the Tutor in English Language and Literature at Magdalen College, Oxford. Besides tutorials he had also to give university lectures. In January 1955 Lewis began his duties (lectures, but no tutorials) at Cambridge as the Professor of Medieval and Renaissance English Literature. This professorial Chair is attached to Magdalene College, Cambridge.]

The great difficulty in comparing my new university with my old is of course that of distinguishing differences between the universities as such from differences between my own life at the one and at the other. My change of allegiance has coincided with change of status. At Oxford I was a busy college teacher; here I am chair-borne. This is an overwhelming change and tends to obliterate every other. Add to this the rejuvenation which any new way of life and any new landscape ordinarily bring to a man in his fifties. These are factors which inevitably distort my vision.

I fly first, therefore, to what is simple, external, and certainly objective. The first and most obvious thing about Cambridge is a glorious negation: we have no Lord Nuffield here.[1] All said and done, we are still a country town. The relief, the liberation, strike me afresh almost every day. In a way it is an eerie relief, for I seem to have recovered the past. Modern Oxford has been not unjustly described as 'the Latin Quarter of Cowley'; Cambridge is very much more like the Oxford I first knew. And here, perhaps, another factor comes in. I was bred at a small college in Oxford; I am now, most gratefully and happily, domiciled in a small college at Cambridge. In between stretch the years in bustling Magdalen, so that this change also makes me feel as if I had been with Aeson in the cauldron. If I were to judge Cambridge and Oxford simply by Magdalen and Magdalene, I should be inclined to say that all I had ever heard of both universities was true except that the

---

[1] In 1913 William Richard Morris (1877–1963), later Lord Nuffield, opened a motor car factory in Cowley which is two miles from the centre of Oxford and about a mile from Lewis's home. From the 1930s onward Morris Motors Ltd has dominated Cowley and made Oxford both a university and an industrial town.

descriptions had somehow got interchanged; that Oxford was progressive, revolutionary, practical, and Cambridge stately, gentle, indulgent, and traditional; that here, not there, we find the last enchantments of the Middle Ages. This would no doubt be too hasty a generalisation. Yet there is some truth in it. Cambridge is more gorgeous. One wears a white tie more often; the feasts are more splendid.

Turning to less ponderable and more important things, I again meet a negation. To me, one of the oddest things about Cambridge is the absence of the philosopher. Of course there have been and are great Cambridge philosophers; indeed contemporary Oxonian philosophy largely represents a successful invasion from Cambridge. But this is apparently quite consistent with the absence of the philosopher. I hardly ever meet a philosopher here. What is even more important, when he is physically absent he does not, as at Oxford, continue to dominate the scene virtually and spiritually. You can talk to Cambridge dons for a whole evening without once hearing the word *quâ*. You can even meet unmistakable classical scholars who don't assume the *Republic* and the *Ethics*[2] as common ground; who behave for all the world as if these (the left and right lung of Oxford humanism) were just two clas-

---

[2] Plato's *Republic* and Aristotle's *Ethics*.

sical texts like any others. It is shocking and refreshing (I never, myself, thought the *Republic* quite deserved its Oxonian status). Later I discovered that there is something at Cambridge which fills the same place philosophy filled at Oxford; a discipline which overflows the faculty of its birth and percolates through all the others and about which the freshman must pick up something if he means to be anybody. This is Literary Criticism (with the largest possible capitals for both words). You were never safe from the philosopher at Oxford; here, never from the Critic.

Everyone asks me what I think about religion at the two universities, so I suppose I must now say something of this subject. As it happens, I have formed a very definite and a very strange impression which may well, as I fully recognise, be premature. I give it for what it may be worth. On the one hand, I think the percentage both of dons and of undergraduates who accept, or even practise, some kind of Christianity is higher at Cambridge than at Oxford. It would be less safe here than there to assume that any man you happened to be talking to was an unbeliever. On the other hand, when unbelief does occur here it seems to be incomparably more militant, more self-conscious, more organised, more interested (even excited) than at Oxford. Over there I know scores of people who did not believe in

the existence of God. But they were no more on their toes
about it than about their disbelief in leprechauns or fly-
ing saucers. The subject hardly ever came up. Their scepticism was relaxed, unemphatic, taken for granted. I doubt
if you could there have founded a society or 'Movement'
based on agreement in that single negative proposition. If
I am right in thinking that atheists are more numerous at
Oxford, this might of course explain their attitude; they
are strong enough to be careless. But I don't feel that this
is the whole truth. I can't help thinking that Oxford scepticism and Cambridge scepticism have different genealo-
gies. I suspect that the Oxonian unbeliever is the son of a
privately unbelieving, externally conforming, nineteenth-
century member of the Church of England; his grandfa-
ther was possibly an archdeacon. Behind his counterpart at
Cambridge I suspect a Unitarian, beyond him a dissenter,
then a Cromwellian, and finally a Puritan of Cartwright's
stamp.[3] He broods (more ambivalently than he suspects)
on persecution—'stern to inflict and stubborn to endure'.

---

[3] Thomas Cartwright (1535–1603), a Puritan divine, was elected in 1550
a scholar of St John's College, Cambridge, which at that time supported
Reformation doctrines. In 1569 he was appointed Lady Margaret
Professor at Cambridge. However, his vigorous criticism of the constitution of the Church of England caused him to lose his professorship. After
a stay in Geneva he took an active part in furthering Presbyterianism and
fostering the Puritan cause.

He is (very properly) much concerned about freedom. He is a keen anti-clerical. Sometimes he seems really to believe that Laud or Mary[4] might at any moment turn up again. To a newcomer from Oxford it is at first a little embarrassing; yet after all, in its way, rather admirable. If ever all this zeal could be directed against those who now really endanger our liberties, it would be of high value. Meanwhile I prefer the fierce to the flippant, who used to be (but is less so now) the characteristically Oxonian plague. For there is a bottomless urbanity that can be very boring.

In 'the manners' as our ancestors would have said—the social climate—I think I begin to discern some differences. But it would be quite misleading to describe these unless I said first, and with all possible emphasis, that they are, on a wide view, infinitesimal. Five minutes' talk with anyone from Redbrick, or from an American or Continental university, will usually make it quite clear that Cambridge and Oxford are far more like one another than either is like anything else in the world. Only an

---

[4] William Laud (1573–1645) when Bishop of St David's conducted a controversy in which he maintained that the Roman Catholic Church and the Church of England are both parts of the same Catholic Church. He became Archbishop of Canterbury in 1633 and his attempts to impose liturgical uniformity aroused the intense hostility of the Puritans. Mary Tudor (1516–1558), daughter of Henry VIII and Catherine of Aragon, became Queen of England in 1553.

eye long familiar with both could see any difference at all; they are like twins whom only their fond parents can tell apart. This is proved by the fact that I now hear told of famous Cambridge 'characters' some of the very same stories I used to hear told of famous Oxford 'characters'; perhaps with equal falsehood, but clearly with equal plausibility, or both. And then there are the characters I have actually met, the 'aged and great' dons—crusty, fruity, 'humourists' (in the old sense), fathomlessly learned, and amidst all their kindness (there's no perfect dish without some sharpness) merciless leg-pullers. This was what I feared I might lose by my migration. I must apologise for my fear; yet what Cambridge man, migrating in the opposite direction, would not have felt it too? It has proved gloriously false; *quod quaeritis hic est,*[5] the pure, cool Oxbridge, the fine flower of humane studies, the thing England has done supremely well.

---

[5] 'What you seek is here.' Why did Lewis use Latin? Owen Barfield thinks he may have intended a 'concealed allusion' to St Matthew 28:5–6. In the *Vulgate* the angel says to the women at the empty tomb *Nolite timere vos scio enim, quod Iesum, qui crucifixus est, quaeritis non est hic* ('Fear not you, for I know that you seek Jesus who was crucified. He is not here'). Miss Nan Dunbar has suggested that Lewis may have had in mind 'an imperfectly remembered phrase' from Horace's *Epistles* I, xi, 29–30. Horace says to Bullatius 'We seek for the good life by means of ships and carriages' but *Quod petis hic est* ('What you seek is here')—*est Ulubrae animus si te non deficit aequis* ('It's at Ulubrae'—i.e., a small, almost deserted town—'if only your composure doesn't desert you').

After the great likeness, the small differences. I think (but this may be accidental and illusory) that the Oxford don, whether in fact married or single, lives more *en garçon* than the Cambridge. You can meet him for a long time in pubs and at High Tables before you are asked to his house. (I have known young foreigners at Oxford who were puzzled and hurt by this.) Oxford has no University Combination Room. Until quite lately—I think I may claim some tiny share in breaking down the tradition—it was unlikely you would meet your female colleagues anywhere except at the Board of the Faculty or at a full dress dinner party. In undergraduate life I think the Junior Common Room counts for more than the Junior Combination Room; but this may vary from college to college.

Of course, not all the similarities between the two universities are desirable ones. I left behind me two evils (or such I think them) at Oxford which I meet again here.

The first needs to be handled with some delicacy, perhaps with more delicacy than I possess, but it is too grave to be passed over in silence. At both places the majority of undergraduates seem to me to be very nice people; much nicer than the pre-1914 vintage as depicted by Sir Compton Mackenzie.[6] But at both there is a minority of

---

[6] In *Sinister Street* (two volumes, 1913–1914).

unhappy young men really very like the 'malcontents' who provide villains for Jacobean drama. They seem to have some grudge or grievance; tense, tight-lipped, hot-eyed, beatle-browed boys, with cheeks as drab, but not so smooth, as putty. They are rude, not with the forgivable *gaucherie* of inexperienced youth (I hate an oldster who is querulous about that; we have all been cubs in our time) but, as it seems, on principle; in the cause of 'integrity' or some other equally detestable virtue. They matter for two reasons. First, they raise a fear that there may be something wrong about our method of intake, or its quantity (academic overproduction is possibly a real danger) or the structure of the educational ladder—in itself an admirable thing. Secondly, I fear that if this type continues it will in the next thirty years prove an extremely disastrous element in our national life. These are future schoolmasters and journalists or, worse still, unemployables with degrees. They could do great harm.

The other evil (in my view) is the incubus of 'Research'. The system was, I believe, first devised to attract the Americans and to emulate the scientists. But the wisest Americans are themselves already sick of it; as one of them said to me, 'I guess we got to come to giving every citizen a Ph. D. shortly after birth, same as baptism and vaccination.' And it is surely clear by now that the needs of the humanities are different from those of the sciences. In science, I gather, a young student fresh from his First in the Tripos can really share in the work of one of his seniors in a way that is useful to himself and even to the subject. But this is not true of the man who has just got his First in English or Modern Languages. Such a man, far from being able or anxious (he is by definition no fool) to add to the sum of human knowledge, wants to acquire a good deal more of the knowledge we already have. He has lately begun to discover how many more things he needs to know in order to follow up his budding interests; that he needs economics, or theology, or philosophy, or archaeology (and always a few more languages). To head him off from these studies, to pinfold him in some small inquiry whose chief claim often is that no one has ever made it before, is cruel and frustrating. It wastes such years as he will never have again; for an old proverb says that 'All the speed is in the morning'. What keeps the system going is the fact that it becomes increasingly difficult to get an academic job without a 'research degree'. Can the two ancient universities do anything by combining to break down this bad usage?

There are other things ... but I call to mind Stevenson's twelfth Fable. It ends, you remember, 'They buried the stranger at the dusk.'

XVIII

IS HISTORY BUNK?

The historical impulse—curiosity about what men thought, did, and suffered in the past—though not universal, seems to be permanent. Different justifications have been found for the works which gratify it. A very simple one is that offered in Barbour's *Bruce;*[1] exciting stories are in any case 'delitabill' and if they happen to be true as well then we shall get a 'doubill pleasance'. More often graver motives are put forward. History is defended as instructive or exemplary: either ethically (the lasting fame or infamy which historians confer upon the dead will teach us to mind our morals) or politically (by seeing how national disasters were brought on in the past we may learn how to avoid them in the future).

As the study of history develops and becomes more like a science these justifications are less confidently advanced.

---

[1] John Barbour (1316?–1395) composed his poem *The Bruce,* celebrating the war of independence and deeds of King Robert and James Douglas, about 1375.

Modern historians are not so ready to classify kings as 'good' and 'bad'. The lessons to be learned by statesmen from past errors become less obvious the more we know. The uniqueness of every historical situation stands out more clearly. In the end most of those who care about history find it safer and franker to admit that they are seeking knowledge of the past (as other men seek knowledge of the nebulae) for its own sake; that they are gratifying a 'liberal' curiosity.

The conception of a 'liberal' curiosity and of the 'liberal' studies which exist to satisfy it is one we owe to Aristotle. 'We call a man *free* whose life is lived for his own sake, not for that of others. In the same way philosophy is of all studies the only *free* one: because it alone exists for its own sake' (*Metaphysics* 982b). Of course *philosophy* does not here mean, as now, the rump or residuum left by the specialisation of the various sciences. And perhaps Aristotle would not, in any case, have allowed the word to cover history (cf. *Poetics* 1451b). That hardly matters. In his conception of a study pursued not for some end beyond itself but for its own sake he has provided most of the activities we carry on at universities with their charter.

Of course this conception (Aristotle meant it only for freemen) has always been baffling and repellent to certain minds. There will always be people who think that any more astronomy than a ship's officer needs for navigation is a waste of time. There will always be those who, on discovering that history cannot really be turned to much practical account, will pronounce history to be Bunk. Aristotle would have called this servile or banausic; we, more civilly, may christen it Fordism.

As the study of history progresses it is almost inevitable, and surely not unreasonable, that partial or departmental histories should arise. The whole past, even within a limited period, becomes too large. Thus we get histories of particular human activities—of law, of shipbuilding, of clothes, of cookery, architecture, or literature. Their justification is the same as that of history *simpliciter* (which, after all, usually meant in effect the history of war and politics). They exist to gratify a liberal curiosity. The knowledge of how men dressed or built or wrote in the past, and why, and why they liked doing it that way, and what it felt like to like that sort of thing, is being sought for its own sake.

Clearly a Fordist view might be taken of these partial histories. It might be maintained that the history of law was legitimate in so far as it yielded practical results: that it studied, or ought to study, 'the valuable' and therefore should notice bad laws and unjust modes of trial only because, and in so far as, those taught us to appreciate more fully the practise of the nineteenth century and therefore to resist more obstinately what seems likely to come upon us in the latter part of the twentieth. This of course is a worthy object. But the claim that legal history depends for its whole right to exist on the performance of such a *corvée* will be granted only by a thorough-going Fordist. We others feel that we should like to know and understand the legal behaviour and legal thought of our ancestors even if no practical gains follow from it.

The departmental history which seems most liable to such attack just at present is the history of literature. Mr Mason said recently in the *Review*, 'It is the study of what is valuable; study of minor figures is only justified if it contributes to the understanding of what is meant by *major*'.[2] Now of course, if we grant that the discipline of literary history is, or can be, or ought to be, merely ancillary to the art of literary criticism, we shall agree with Mr Mason. But why should we grant this?

Let us be quite clear what the question is. If a man says, 'I have no interest in the history of literature simply as history', one would have no controversy with him. One would reply, 'Well, I dare say not; don't let me detain you.'

---

[2] H. A. Mason, 'Churchill's Satire', a review of *The Poetical Works of Charles Churchill*, ed. Douglas Grant (1956) in *The Cambridge Review*, vol. LXXVIII (11 May 1957), p. 571.

If he says, 'I think criticism twenty times more important than any knowledge of the past', one would say, 'No doubt that is quite a reasonable view.' If he said, 'Literary history is not criticism', I should heartily agree. That indeed is my point. The study of the forms and styles and sentiments of past literature, the attempt to understand how and why they evolved as they did, and (if possible) by a sort of instructed empathy to re-live momentarily in ourselves the tastes for which they catered, seems to me as legitimate and liberal as any other discipline; even to be one without which our knowledge of man will be very defective. Of course it is not a department of criticism; it is a department of a department of history (*Kulturgeschichte*). As such it has its own standing. It is not to be judged by the use it may or may not happen to have for those whose interests are purely critical.

Of course I would grant (and so, I expect, would Mr Mason) that literary history and criticism can overlap. They usually do. Literary historians nearly always allow themselves some valuations, and literary critics nearly always commit themselves to some historical propositions. (To describe an element in Donne's poetry as new commits you to the historical proposition that it is not to be found in previous poetry.) And I would agree (if that is part of what he means) that this overlap creates a danger of confusions. Literary (like constitutional) historians can be betrayed into thinking that when they have traced the evolution of a thing they have somehow proved its worth; literary critics may be unaware of the historical implications (often risky) which lurk in their evaluative criticism.

But if Mr Mason is denying literary history's right to exist, if he is saying that no one must study the past of literature except as a means of criticism, I think his position is far from self-evident and ought to be supported. And I think he is denying that. For if one values literary history as history, it is of course very clear why we study bad work as well as good. To the literary historian a bad, though once popular, poem is a challenge; just as some apparently irrational institution is a challenge to the political historian. We want to know how such stuff came to be written and why it was applauded; we want to understand the whole *ethos* which made it attractive. We are, you see, interested in men. We do not demand that everyone should share our interests.

The whole question invites further discussion. But I think that discussion will have to begin further back. Aristotle's (or Newman's) whole conception of the liberal may have to be questioned. Fordism may admit of some brilliant defence. We may have to ask whether literary criticism is itself an end or a means and, if a means, to what. But till all this has been canvassed I was unwilling that the case for literary history should go by default. We cannot, pending a real discussion, let pass the assumption that this species of history, any more than others, is to be condemned unless it can deliver some sort of 'goods' for present use.

XIX

SEX IN LITERATURE

I am told that one of the causes which led to the abandonment of our older penal code was the fact that as juries grew more humane they simply refused to convict. The evidence showed beyond doubt that the famished girl in the dock had stolen a handkerchief. But they didn't want her to be hanged for that, so they returned a verdict of Not Guilty.

That people were no longer hanged for trivial offences was obviously a change for the better. But patently false verdicts were not the best way of bringing that change about. It is a bad thing that the results of trials should depend on the personal moral philosophy of a particular jury rather than on what has been proved in court. For one thing, that procedure, though it may lead to mercy in one case, may have the opposite effect in another.

The moral seems to me to be clear. When the prevalent morality of a nation comes to differ unduly from that presupposed in its laws, the laws must sooner or later change and conform to it. And the sooner they do so the better. For till they do we inevitably have humbug, perjury, and confusion.

This applies equally whether prevalent morality is departing from that embodied in the laws for the better or for the worse. The law must rise to our standards when we improve and sink to them when we decay. It is a lesser evil that the laws should sink than that all judicial procedure should become a travesty.

If we ceased to disapprove of murder, we should, no doubt, be fools and villains. But it would be better to admit the fact and alter the law accordingly than to go on acquitting of murder those who had certainly committed it.

But this, I believe, is the actual situation as regards 'obscene' or 'corrupting' literature. The older law—for compromise has now begun—embodied a morality for which masturbation, perversion, fornication, and adultery were great evils. It therefore, not illogically, discountenanced the publication of books which seemed likely to encourage these modes of behaviour.

The morality of the modern intelligentsia—who supply 'expert witnesses'—is different. If it were fully and frankly stated it would, I believe, run as follows: 'We are not sure that these things are evils at all, and we are quite sure that they are not the sort of evils the law ought to be concerned with.'

My own view—just to get it out of the way—is that they are evils, but that the law should be concerned with none of them except adultery. Adultery is an affair for law because it offends the Hobbesian principle 'that men perform their covenants'. The fact that this particular breach of covenant involves the sexual act is (in the logical sense) an accident.

But I am not here arguing my own view. What I want is a straight fight between the new morality and that of the law. Do not be alarmed, my fellow authors; your side will almost certainly win.

In the meantime the situation is most unsatisfactory. Behind much discussion, and even behind the recent modification of the law, there hover two propositions that I think far less admissible than the new morality:

(1) That if a book is real 'literature' it cannot corrupt. But there is no evidence for this, and some against it. No one can predict what may inflame adolescents, any more than what may frighten children; I have heard of the most improbable results as regards both. This is a stock argument against forbidding certain books. But it is equally an argument against this particular plea for tolerating them.

(2) That if a book is a great 'work of art' it doesn't matter whether it corrupts or not, because art matters more than behaviour. In other words, art matters more than life; comment on life, or the mirroring of life, more than life itself. This sounds very like nonsense.

Whatever happens we don't want anything like the Lady Chatterley case again.[1] Now that the (strangely savage) yells of triumph are dying down, it may be suggested that this was not an affair to feel very proud of. I don't mean because of the verdict. I think it mattered very little either to our literature or to our morals how it was decided. It is the conduct of the case that disquiets me.

What was really at issue? The jury were told from the bench that 'we are not sitting here as judges of taste' (p. 27 in Mr Rolph's account). They were told later by counsel that they were 'not concerned with a question of personal good taste' (p. 35). Yet in fact nearly all the witnesses were examined at great length on the literary merits of the book. How would you define *taste* so as to make literary merits not a question of taste?

---

[1] The publication of D. H. Lawrence's *Lady Chatterley's Lover* by Penguin Books in 1960 was the subject of the case *Regina v. Penguin Books Limited* at the Old Bailey during 20 October–2 November 1960. The case resulted in the acquittal of Penguin Books. A transcript of what was said at the trial was published under the title *The Trial of Lady Chatterley*, ed. C. H. Rolph (Penguin Books, 1961).

Again, these witnesses are summoned as 'experts'. The implication is that there are 'experts' in literature in the same sense in which there are experts in engineering or medicine.

Now I am not at all suggesting that literature is a realm in which anyone's opinion is as good as anyone else's. Most undoubtedly the judgements of ripe critics should be heard with great respect. The point is that they are judgements, not statements about matters of fact. They are all reversible.

Anyone familiar with literary history knows that an almost unanimous critical opinion may prove transient. Think where Scott and Byron were once placed. I should like some assurance that the distinction between literary 'experts' and expert witnesses ordinarily so called was clear in the minds of the jury.

The Bishop of Woolwich appears to have been cited as an expert in the general nature of good and evil.[2] It may be, for all I know, that his wisdom and sanctity qualify him for this prophetic role. But the qualification mentioned in court was that he had read ethics.

---

[2] The Bishop of Woolwich was the Rt Rev. J. A. T. Robinson. Bishop Robinson said of the adulterous 'sex relationship' in *Lady Chatterley's Lover:* 'I think Lawrence tried to portray this relation as in a real sense something sacred, as in a real sense an act of holy communion', *The Trial of Lady Chatterley*, p. 71.

So have I and a good many others. I don't think that discipline qualifies us to say what is or is not 'sacred' more than other men. A witness put forward to tell the jury, as an expert, what is right or wrong strikes at the roots of trial by jury. Its presupposition is that twelve good men and true know that already.

The lesser of the evils now before us is to abandon all moral censorship. We have either sunk beneath or risen above it. If we do, there will be reams of filth. But we need not read it. Nor, probably, will the fashion last for ever. Four-letter words may soon be as dated as antimacassars.

DISCOVER C. S. LEWIS

Introducing the *C. S. Lewis* Signature Classics
Eight Key Titles Presented Together for the First Time

HARDCOVER GIFT EDITION

PAPERBACK ANTHOLOGY

EIGHT-VOLUME BOX SET

Mere Christianity • The Screwtape Letters • Miracles • The Great Divorce
The Problem of Pain • A Grief Observed • The Abolition of Man • The Four Loves